Truth in Religion

Truth in Religion

THE PLURALITY OF RELIGIONS
AND THE UNITY OF TRUTH

An Essay in the Philosophy of Religion

Mortimer J. Adler

MACMILLAN PUBLISHING COMPANY · NEW YORK

COLLIER MACMILLAN CANADA · TORONTO

MAXWELL MACMILLAN INTERNATIONAL

NEW YORK · OXFORD · SINGAPORE · SYDNEY

Macmillan Publishing Company
866 Third Avenue, New York, NY 10022

Collier Macmillan Canada, Inc.
1200 Eglinton Avenue East, Suite 200
Don Mills, Ontario M3C 3N1

Library of Congress Cataloging-in-Publication Data
Adler, Mortimer Jerome, ———
        Truth in religion : the plurality of religions and the unity of
    truth : an essay in the philosophy of religion / Mortimer J. Adler.
            p.   cm.
        ISBN 0-02-500225-2
        1. Religion.   2. Truth.   3. Religious pluralism.   I. Title.
    BL50.A35   1990
    200'.1—dc20   90-32840   CIP

Macmillan books are available at special discounts for bulk purchases for sales promotions, premiums, fund-raising, or educational use.
For details, contact:

    Special Sales Director
    Macmillan Publishing Company
    866 Third Avenue
    New York, NY 10022

10 9 8 7 6 5 4 3 2 1

Printed in the United States of America

CONTENTS

v

PREFACE

FOR many years I have been concerned with cultural pluralism and for the need to restrict it to matters where such pluralism is desirable as well as unavoidable. That is why I have included in this volume as appendices excerpts from three lectures given at earlier dates.

One was a lecture I delivered in 1973 at the Aspen Institute. The question had been raised whether Far Eastern great books should be included in the list of readings for the seminars being conducted in Aspen, along with the great books in the tradition of Western civilization. The lecture was, in part, my effort to explain the reasons for my emphatically negative answer.

The second appended lecture was delivered in Tokyo at International House in 1978 to an audience of scholars, scientists, and philosophers from the local universities as well as leading businessmen. I called the attention of that audience to the conflict between two spheres of thought in some Far Eastern cultures: on the one hand their trust in Western technology and in the soundness of its underlying mathematics and physics; on the other hand their devotion to their religious beliefs and practices. Were they content, I asked, to keep these two commitments in logic-tight compartments and so prevent them from challenging each other? Were they not disturbed by the apparent schizophrenia that they suffered in consequence of this? They were, I discovered from the discussion thereafter, quite content, quite undisturbed.

The third appendix is of more recent date although it is a summation of many lectures that I have given at Aspen in the last twenty-five years. I delivered this one in July of 1989. The excerpts chosen from that lecture deal especially with the sameness of human nature at all times and places and with the sameness of the human mind wherever we find human beings.

In 1981, when I wrote the chapters on truth in *Six Great Ideas*, I further developed the distinction between matters of taste, with respect to which pluralism is desirable, and matters of truth, with respect to which it is not; and I raised the question whether philosophy and religion belonged to the sphere of taste or to the sphere of truth.

I call attention to these earlier lectures and to the chapters on truth in *Six Great Ideas* because some of the things said there are repeated in this book in order to make advances that were not made in these earlier materials.

The advances were provoked by four recent books, two on mythology, one by Professor Wendy Doniger O'Flaherty entitled *Other Peoples' Myths*, the other by Professor Joseph Campbell entitled *The Inner Reaches of Outer Space*. Both books have a bearing on the question of truth in religion.

The other two books are directly concerned with where truth lies among the plurality of religions. One of these is by Professor Harvey Cox entitled *Many Mansions*, the other is by Father Hans Küng entitled *Theology for the Third Millennium: An Ecumenical View*. I have dealt with the views of O'Flaherty and Campbell in Chapter 3, and with the views of Cox and Küng in Chapter 4.

Having explained the background of this book by referring to the three appendices and also what motivated me to write it, I now wish to provide a brief outline of the chapters that constitute the book itself.

The title of this book indicates that its two main subjects are the plurality of religions and the unity of truth. Hence I begin in Chapter 1 with a discussion of pluralism and what restrictions must be imposed upon it when we are concerned with matters of truth as differentiated from matters of taste —matters in which the diversity of opinions and preferences must be acknowledged, and accepted without argument. Everyone is familiar with the maxim *De gustibus non disputandum est*: about matters of taste, there is no disputing. But not everyone is familiar with the maxim *De veritate disputandum est*: about matters of truth, we should engage in dispute— that is, we should have recourse to the effort to reach agreement about what is true and false.

Chapter 2 sets forth the logical considerations that underlie one's engagement in the pursuit of truth in any field in which persons claim truth for their views, their doctrines, or their beliefs. Readers will find there a full explanation of what is involved in the separation of matters of truth from matters of taste as well as the argument for the unity of truth against those who think that incompatible views, doctrines, or beliefs can be embraced as true.

In Chapter 3, concerning the study of religion, a working definition of religion will be advanced and criteria will be

PREFACE

proposed for classifying the major world religions in existence today. Almost all of them, if not all, make claims for the truth of their beliefs—the prescriptive truth of their moral precepts or the descriptive, factual truth of their credal commitments, or both. In some religions, credal commitments may not be explicitly expressed, but they are always implicitly presupposed by claims for the truth of prescriptive moral precepts. It is in this context that mythology is discussed in relation to religion, and their difference is illuminated by the distinction between poetical truth and logical truth, descriptive or prescriptive.

Chapter 4 deals with the difficult problem of where the truth lies in the plurality of religions that not only differ from one another but make incompatible claims about the truth of their beliefs concerning God, the cosmos, and human nature, as well as about the truth of their prescriptions concerning how human beings should conduct their lives. It is there that the unity of truth comes into play in dealing with the plurality of religions that make incompatible claims of truth. The book ends, in Chapter 5, with questions to be answered rather than with answers, with issues to be resolved rather than with their resolution.

I must caution readers that I have written this book as a philosopher and not as a communicant of one of the world's great religions. It is, therefore, not a piece of apologetics, arguing for the truth of one religion as opposed to others. It attempts to clarify the problem of truth in religion, but it does not attempt to solve it. In my judgment, the clarification it provides is a step toward the solution.

Finally, I must express my indebtedness to Otto Bird, associated with me for many years at the Institute for Philosophical Research, for all the help he has given me in the preparation and writing of this book; to John Van Doren, also

PREFACE

my colleague at the Institute, for his advice and assistance; to Professor Wendy Doniger O'Flaherty of the University of Chicago Divinity School, for the helpful conversations we had about mythology and religion; and to my secretary, Marlys Allen, for her patience in dealing with the revision of the manuscript.

Truth in Religion

CHAPTER 1

The Restriction of Pluralism

(i)

Pluralism, tolerance, and liberalism (the kind of liberalism that is doctrinaire) are twentieth-century terms that have a few antecedents in modern thought, especially in that of the nineteenth century, but they have none in antiquity and the Middle Ages.

The doctrinaire liberals of the twentieth century espouse pluralism and tolerance as if they were desirable values on which no restrictions or qualifications should be placed when they are applied to the life of society and of thought. They reveal thereby their lack of understanding of what should be for them a seminal and formative work, John Stuart Mill's great essay *On Liberty*, especially its chapter on freedom of thought and discussion.

Pluralism is a desirable policy in all realms of action and thought *except* those in which unity is required. When unity is required, pluralism must be restricted. For example, a stable and peaceful society cannot exist under the domination of two or more competing governments unless one is subordinate to the other. The structure of a federal government, such as that of the United States, with the major sovereignty being vested in the national government and purely internal sovereignty being vested in the state governments, affords us with an example of restricted political pluralism that works effectively. Also, an effective and viable economy cannot be organized by competing and opposed economic principles. In the political realm, this does not exclude the pluralism of competing political parties; in the economic realm, it does not exclude the pluralism of competing entrepreneurial agencies. In both cases, the desirable pluralism is subordinate to a controlling unity.

It may seem odd to associate a choice between competing political parties, or the favoring of one or another entrepreneurial agency in the marketplace, with preference in matters of taste among diverse cuisines or styles of dress. However, wherever reasonable men can reasonably disagree, as they can about questions of political expediency or about economic options, their decision in favor of one or another alternative is a preference that closely resembles preferences in what are more obviously matters of taste.

(ii)

In the sphere of all matters subject to individual thought and decision, pluralism is desirable and tolerable only in those areas that are matters of taste rather than matters of truth. Preferences with regard to cuisine, dress, patterns of dance, social manners, artistic styles, do not raise any questions of truth. Where that is the case, pluralism has always existed on earth, not only in different societies and cultures, but sometimes also within a single society or culture. When, within a single society or culture, the attempt is made to regiment the conduct of individuals with respect to matters of taste, that regimentation aims at a monolithic control of individual preferences and decisions.

The reaction against such monolithic or totalitarian regimentation is the motivating force of liberalism's spirited defense of toleration for diversity in all matters where individuals have a right to be free in expressing and acting on personal preference. Such matters belong in the sphere of the voluntary. But with regard to matters that belong in the sphere of intellect, matters involving truth not taste, a persistent pluralism is intolerable.

The mind of any one individual engaged in the pursuit of truth is necessitated in the judgments it makes by whatever mass of evidence or weight of reasons point in one direction rather than another. The affirmative judgment that this proposition (i.e., that atoms are fissionable) is true rather than the opposite is intellectually necessitated.

At that point, one cannot tolerate being open-minded about the excluded alternatives. But such intolerance is entirely a private matter. It does not call for the suppression of the false opinions that others may still hold. It does not call for any social or political action enforcing unanimity in the adoption of the truth. It does not call for witch hunts, McCarthy tactics, or the burning of heretics. It calls only for continued discussion between individuals.

Some of the matters about which we are obliged to think and act are *not* matters of taste. Only with regard to matters of taste and public policy should individual freedom to differ be preserved and should recourse to voting be considered. There

3

is another realm, concerned with questions of truth, in which unity is required and in which pluralism is out of place. In history, mathematics, science, and philosophy there is room for competing and conflicting theories, hypotheses, doctrines, or propositions, *only as long as no one of them is, at a given time, established as true.*

I stress the reference to a given time because the pursuit of truth is an ongoing process in which the judgment of what is true and false changes from time to time. This does not alter the fact that, *at a given time,* judgments concerning which of two or more competing alternatives is true are exclusionary judgments. For the time being, other alternatives are ruled out as false.

This applies to judgments about questions of value as well as to judgments about matters of fact. To view pluralism in regard to values as desirable and tolerable is tantamount to dismissing all value judgments as matters of taste rather than as matters of truth. If, however, the prescriptive judgments we make about how to conduct our lives and our communities—judgments that contain the word "ought"—can be true or false, then they are subject to the unity of truth, as much so as our judgments in mathematics and empirical science.

There is another way of assigning certain matters to the sphere of truth and certain matters to the sphere of taste. Anything that is transcultural is clearly in the sphere of truth. Anything that is not—*and should not be*—transcultural is in the sphere of taste. That leaves open questions about matters that at this juncture in history are not transcultural but, perhaps, should be.

There is no question that technology and its underlying mathematics and science are transcultural. There is no question about cuisine, style in dress, social manners, and the like.

They are not transcultural and should not be. But what about philosophy? Religion?

Though at present philosophy is not transcultural, my understanding of the role of philosophy among the disciplines of learning leads me to think it should become transcultural. As I hope will become clear later, it can do so by passing the test of truth that consists in its being compatible with the knowledge available through the work of the empirical sciences.

Like philosophy, religion at the present is not transcultural, but that leaves quite open the question whether it should be. The answer to that question depends, in my judgment, on the relation of religion to philosophy, on the one hand, and to mythology, on the other. The resolution of the issues concerning these two relationships will be found, I hope, in the third and fourth chapters of this book.

(iii)

I have used the words "tolerable" and "intolerable" in referring to matters where individual freedom of preference or decision should be allowed, as distinguished from those matters where the intellect, in its pursuit of truth, is obliged to try to overcome pluralism and to achieve unity.

In his chapter on freedom of thought and discussion, Mill is concerned with the pursuit of truth. With truth as the ultimate goal to be achieved, he advocates the toleration of competing doctrines and opinions so that, when all are fairly considered and submitted to arguments pro and con, the truth is more likely to be discovered.

Mill advocates the toleration of individuals who differ in thought and speech, but not tolerance for competing doctrines or opinions, as if they were all equally acceptable or preferable. He does not look upon pluralism with respect to matters of truth in the same way that he looks upon pluralism with respect to matters of taste. Readers should consult the note appended to this chapter in order to understand how Mill's views about liberty of thought and discussion are affected by his concern with the pursuit of truth.

So far I have not mentioned religion. For those who regard religion as not belonging to the realm of truth, there is no problem about pluralism any more than there is a problem about pluralism with regard to cuisine, dress, style, and so on. Only if, with regard to the diversity of religions, there are questions about truth and falsehood do we have a problem about the pluralism of religions and the unity of truth.

That problem is not concerned with preserving religious liberty, freedom of worship, and the toleration, in a particular society or in the world, of a diversity of religious institutions, communities, practices, and beliefs. It is concerned only with the question of where, in that diversity, the truth lies if there is any truth in religion at all.

Note to Chapter 1

Here are some crucial passages on liberty of thought and discussion in Chapter 2 of J. S. Mill's essay *On Liberty*.

> But the peculiar evil of silencing the expression of an opinion is, that it is robbing the human race; posterity as well as the existing generation; those who dissent from the opinion, still more than those who hold it. If the opinion is right, they are deprived of the opportunity of exchanging error for truth: if wrong, they lose, what is almost as great a benefit, the clearer perception and livelier impression of truth, produced by its collision with error.

> ———

> The highest aim and best result of improved intelligence, it has hitherto been thought, is to unite mankind more and more in the acknowledgment of all important truths; and does the intelligence only last as long as it has not achieved its object? Do the fruits of conquest perish by the very completeness of the victory?
>
> I affirm no such thing. As mankind improve, the number of doctrines which are no longer disputed or doubted will be constantly on the increase: and the well-being of mankind may almost be measured by the number and gravity of the truths which have reached the point of being uncontested. . . . But though this gradual narrowing of the bounds of diversity of opinion is necessary in both senses of the term, being at once inevitable and indispensable, we are

not therefore obliged to conclude that all its consequences must be beneficial. The loss of so important an aid to the intelligent and living apprehension of a truth, as is afforded by the necessity of explaining it to, or defending it against, opponents, though not sufficient to outweigh, is no trifling drawback from, the benefit of its universal recognition. Where this advantage can no longer be had, I confess I should like to see the teachers of mankind endeavouring to provide a substitute for it; some contrivance for making the difficulties of the question as present to the learner's consciousness, as if they were pressed upon him by a . . . [dissident] champion, eager for his conversion.

But instead of seeking contrivances for this purpose, they have lost those they formerly had. The Socratic dialectics, so magnificently exemplified in the dialogues of Plato, were a contrivance of this description. They were essentially a negative discussion of the great questions of philosophy and life, directed with consummate skill to the purpose of convincing any one who had merely adopted the commonplaces of received opinion that he did not understand the subject—that he as yet attached no definite meaning to the doctrines he professed; in order that, becoming aware of his ignorance, he might be put in the way to obtain a stable belief, resting on a clear apprehension both of the meaning of doctrines and of their evidence. The school disputations of the Middle Ages had a somewhat similar object. They were intended to make sure that the pupil understood his own opinion, and (by necessary correlation) the opinion opposed to it, and could enforce the grounds of the one and confute those of the other.

We have now recognised the necessity to the mental well-being of mankind (on which all their other well-being depends) of freedom of opinion, and freedom of the expression of opinion, on four distinct grounds; which we will now briefly recapitulate.

First, if any opinion is compelled to silence, that opinion may, for aught we can certainly know, be true. To deny this is to assume our own infallibility.

Secondly, though the silenced opinion be an error, it may, and very commonly does, contain a portion of truth; and since the general or prevailing opinion on any subject is rarely or never the whole truth, it is only by the collision of adverse opinions that the remainder of the truth has any chance of being supplied.

Thirdly, even if the received opinion be not only true, but the whole truth; unless it is suffered to be, and actually is, vigorously and earnestly contested, it will, by most of those who receive it, be held in the manner of a prejudice, with little comprehension or feeling of its rational grounds. And not only this, but fourthly, the meaning of the doctrine itself will be in danger of being lost, or enfeebled, and deprived of its vital effect on the character and conduct: the dogma becoming a mere formal profession, inefficacious for good, but cumbering the ground, and preventing the growth of any real and heartfelt conviction, from reason or personal experience.

CHAPTER 2

The Logic of Truth

(i)

The logic of truth is the same for all exclusionary claims to truth—claims that something is correctly judged to be true and that all judgments to the contrary are, therefore, incorrect. The proposition may be a theorem in mathematics, a scientific generalization, a conclusion of historical research, a philosophical principle, or an article of religious faith.

For simplicity's sake, I focus on a single proposition. The point I have just made remains unaltered when we consider sets of conjoined propositions that constitute systematic theories, hypotheses, or doctrines. If any one proposition in a set of conjoined propositions is false, the set as a whole is false, but its falsity can be corrected by the elimination of the false proposition from the set.

There is, however, one use of the word "truth" to which what I have just said does not apply. People use the phrase "poetical truth" and apply it to functional narratives—stories, novels, plays. Several stories about the same characters can be told. They may differ in this or that detail, as do the three Electra plays by Aeschylus, Sophocles, and Euripides. But the fact that they differ does not prevent them all from being poetically true. The three plays are not opposed to one another in such a way that if one is poetically true, the other two are poetically false.

In the sphere of fine arts where taste reigns supreme, poetical truth prevails. One novel or play, one painting, one piece of music does not replace another, nor does it correct mistakes made in other works, as one scientific theory or one philosophical doctrine replaces another by virtue of its superior claim to truth or by correcting errors to be found in the other theories or doctrines. The pluralism that is intellectually intolerable in the sphere of logical truth is quite tolerable in the sphere of poetical truth. If, for example, myths have poetical, not logical, truth, then all can be true, one not excluding others; but if logical truth were claimed for any one of them, that would exclude claims for the truth of other, incompatible myths. That myths do not have logical truth is manifest in the fact that myths are never incompatible with one another. The same can be said of works of fine art.

With the exception of novels that claim to be historical fiction, fictional narratives tell stories but do not make explicit assertions. They do not affirm or deny the truth of propositions. Therefore, the logic of truth with which we are here concerned does not apply to them. My reason for saying that poetical truth can be a property of fictional narratives is that this may be the kind of truth that belongs to myths and to religions, in which case the logic of truth does not apply to myths and religions. I shall return to this possibility in Chapters 3 and 4.

In what follows I shall use the phrase "logical truth" to

signify the kind of truth that belongs to propositions or judgments, descriptive or prescriptive, that are subject to contradiction. Such truth, if descriptive, is factual truth, giving us knowledge of the observed phenomena or of reality. If prescriptive, it is a normative truth about goods to be sought or actions to be done.

In contrast, I shall use the phrase "poetical truth" to signify the kind of truth that is not subject to contradiction, the kind of truth that belongs to narratives that, though differing, are in no way incompatible with one another. The line that divides fact from fiction and fantasy also divides logical from poetical truth.

(ii)

The logic of truth requires us to distinguish between (1) a proposition entertained with suspended judgment and (2) a proposition judged—that is, asserted to be either true or false. The truth or falsity of entertained propositions is absolute and immutable. The correctness of the judgments we make about them is relative and mutable. The failure to make this distinction leads to such unguarded and incorrect statements as "This may be true for you but it is not true for me, and that is all there is to it," or "This once was true, but it is no longer true and that is all there is to it."

To be guarded and correct, what should have been said is "The judgment you make about it may be correct in your eyes, but as I view the matter, it is not correct, but that is not all there is to it, because the proposition we are judging differently is either true or false absolutely without any regard for our differences of opinion about it."

Similarly, with regard to past and present, what should have been said to be guarded and correct is "The judgment made in the past about the proposition was once correct; now it is no longer correct; but that is not all there is to it, because the proposition itself was false then as it is now, even though it was incorrectly judged to be true then."

One example should suffice to make this clear. The proposition "atoms, the smallest particles of matter, are indivisible" was, in the history of Western science from Democritus in antiquity to the end of the nineteenth century, thought to be true by all eminent physicists without exception. Only in the twentieth century do all physicists make the opposite judgment, declaring it to be false. The experimental evidence supports the correctness of the present judgment and indicates that the earlier judgment was incorrect. But the proposition itself, the proposition as entertained by the mind, was always false. It did not become false in the twentieth century because the correct judgment about it was finally made.[1]

(iii)

One might give many more such examples from history of the natural sciences or from stages in the development of historical research about past events, but more examples are not needed for an understanding of the point being made. However, it

---

1. A fuller exposition of this theory of truth is to be found in my book *Six Great Ideas* (New York, 1981), Chapters 5 and 6. The reader will also find there the refutation of both extreme and moderate skepticism about the existence and objectivity of truth.

might be useful to give an example from the field of philosophical theology.

In antiquity, the proposition that the cosmos or universe
exists everlastingly, without beginning or end, was judged
true by Aristotle. In the Middle Ages, that same proposition
was judged false by Aquinas because it was incompatible with
one article of Christian faith, namely, that in the beginning
God created heaven and earth and that this creation *ab initio*
was also *ex nihilo*. In twentieth-century cosmology, still a
different proposition is judged to be true; namely, that the
world began about fifteen billion years ago with the Big Bang.
Without saying which of these judgments is correct, we can
say without hesitation that all three of the propositions here
being entertained can be false, but if one of them is true, it
always was and always will be true and the other two, being
incompatible with it, always were and always will be false.

The general public has been misled by contemporary physicists into thinking that they have the right answer to the
question of the beginning of the universe, and of time also,
with the Big Bang. The physicists confuse themselves as well
as others by converting what is not measurable by them into
being nonexistent in reality. Whatever banged at the beginning of measurable time—the time measurable by physicists
—preexisted that momentous event in a period of time not
accessible to physical measurement. Moreover, if the creation
of the cosmos is identical with its exnihilation, the physicists'
Big Bang cannot qualify as creation. It is not the beginning
of anything except physically measurable time. Stephen Hawking's *A Brief History of Time* was mistitled; it should have
been *A Brief History of Measurable Time*.[2]

---

2. See Stanley L. Jaki, *God and the Cosmologists* (Washington, DC, 1990).

THE LOGIC OF TRUTH

The logic of incompatible propositions is formulated by modern logicians in a manner that is slightly different from the way it was treated in antiquity. Aristotle, for example, distinguished incompatible propositions that are contradictory from incompatible propositions that are only contrary.

In the case of contradictories, no middle ground is possible. The theistic affirmation *God exists* and the atheistic denial *God does not exist* stand in contradiction to one another: both cannot be true and both cannot be false; if one is true, the other must be false.

The opposition of propositions that are contraries, not contradictories, is a weaker opposition; and a middle ground is possible. The monotheistic affirmation that there is only one God and the polytheistic affirmation that there are many gods cannot both be true, but both can be false. The atheist may be right that neither God nor gods exist.

Modern logicians speak in terms of strong and weak disjunctions. A strong disjunction is like the opposition of contradictories: either the proposition P is true or the proposition not-P is true, but both cannot be true and both cannot be false. In contrast, a weak disjunction is like the opposition of contraries: either P or not-P is true, but both can be false. Here a middle ground is possible. For example, the two generalizations, *All swans are white* and *No swans are white* cannot both be true; if one is true, the other must be false; but both can be false, as they are when the truth lies in the middle ground: *Some swans are white* and *Some swans are not white*.

Subsequently, when we are concerned with the truth of opposed religious beliefs, the kind of opposition with which we will mainly deal is that of contrariety (or weak disjunction), not that of contradiction (or strong disjunction). If one of the opposed beliefs is true, the other cannot be true, but both may be false.

15

Only occasionally will we be confronted with contradictions or strong disjunctions of the kind indicated above, which occur between the theist and the atheist, one affirming and the other denying the existence of a single divinity or of a plurality of deities.

I should add that the disproof of a proposition can be accomplished either by the proof of its contrary or of its contradictory. Strong disjunction or contradiction is not necessary for disproof.

(iv)

When we employ the adjectives "certain" and "probable" as if some propositions were certainly true and others only probably true, we are speaking incorrectly. These two adjectives apply properly to our judgments about what is true but not to the truth of entertained propositions. An entertained proposition is just true or false. Since no judgment about it is being made, certitude and doubt do not apply at all.

Only those of our judgments that are made beyond a shadow of a doubt are made with certitude. We make few such judgments. Most of our judgments fall within the shadow of doubt. The two degrees of uncertainty attaching to them and making our judgments only probable are the two degrees employed by judicial tribunals in the trial of issues of fact, either beyond a reasonable doubt or by a preponderance of the evidence.

We are concerned here only with the truth of entertained propositions, not with the correctness or incorrectness, and not with the certitude or degree of probability, of our judgments about their truth. Hence much that occupies the attention of methodologists who consider how to test the

16

correctness of our judgments about the truth of entertained propositions, or who consider how to determine the probability of such judgments, need not delay us. But the mention of these considerations does lead us to a point of the greatest importance in our effort to apply the logic of truth to religion.

The ascertainment of correct judgments about which entertained propositions are true and which are false involves quite different procedures in such diverse fields as mathematics and history, or physics and metaphysics. In these different fields of study or inquiry, the criteria employed and the methods used for testing the correctness of our judgments differ. Yet the logic applied to the entertained truths that are being judged in these different fields is exactly the same despite the differences that exist in the criteria and methods employed in ascertaining the correctness of our judgments.

(v)

What is common to entertained propositions in all different fields of empirical and rational inquiry is the fact that the propositions being judged and the judgments we make about them can have or lack the support of evidence and reasons. Using the word "proof" loosely to refer to all the ways in which the assemblage of evidence and the marshaling of reasons can be used to support the correctness of the judgment that the proposition being entertained is true, we can say that proof is common to all the different fields of empirical and rational inquiry.

Here religion differs radically. The propositions entertained as true in religious creeds or in articles of religious faith are entirely beyond proof. Regardless of whether the judgment made about their truth is correct or incorrect, its correctness cannot be ascertained by any conceivable mode of empirical research or rational inquiry.

The affirmation, as the result of rational argument, that God exists is a conclusion of philosophical theology. Belief in God, creator of heaven and earth, and of all things visible and invisible, is an article of Christian faith, proclaimed in the Nicene Creed.[3] It is also an article of faith in Judaism and Islam.

According to Thomas Aquinas, the philosophical argument proving God's existence is essentially a preamble to faith; but he also says that accidentally or under certain circumstances, it can also be an article of faith for those who are unable to follow the argument that reaches the conclusion affirming God's existence.

Aquinas, in addition, calls our attention to those articles of Christian faith (also enunciated in the Nicene Creed) that are beliefs to which *all* faithful Christians subscribe, unlike the belief in God's existence, which is an article of faith *only* for those unable to follow the rational argument to its conclusion.[4] These articles consist of beliefs in the unprovable propositions that state the great mysteries of Christian theology, such as the triune nature of the godhead and the incarnation of God in the dual nature of the person Jesus Christ.

Much earlier than Aquinas, Tertullian had declared *"Credo*

---

3. In my book *How to Think About God* (New York, 1980), written for pagans by a pagan, the purely philosophical proof of God's existence is set forth: and the chasm between the God proved philosophically and the God believed in by the faithful is clear. That chasm can only be crossed by a leap of faith.

4. The philosophical argument for God's existence establishes a conclusion affirming God's existence beyond a reasonable doubt. But this philosophical affirmation falls short of the religious belief in God, not only as creator of the cosmos but also as providentially concerned with man's destiny. This is an article of faith even for those who can understand the philosophical argument for God's existence.

quia absurdium est" (I believe because it is absurd); that is, because that which I believe cannot rationally be proved, what I believe can be affirmed only by an act of religious faith.

In what follows, I shall be concerned only with those beliefs in Judaism, Christianity, Islam, and all other religions that lie totally beyond the sphere of rational argument. While such articles of faith cannot be proved or disproved, I will explain presently how they can be tested, and, should they fail the test, be discredited.

Let me illustrate this point with respect to three religions of the West—Judaism, Christianity, and Islam. Christian theologians hold that the affirmation of God's existence is not an article of faith for all Christians but only for some—those who are not persuaded by rational argument. They do so precisely because they think, correctly or incorrectly, that God's existence can be proved by reason. Those who make the opposite, the agnostic, judgment, make God's existence an article of faith precisely because they think the proposition that God exists cannot be proved, and that it lies totally beyond the realm of our natural knowledge.

It is an article of Jewish faith that, on Mt. Sinai, Moses received from God the ten commandments engraved on the stone tablets. That belief is based on the belief in the truth of the five books of Moses in the Old Testament. Regardless of whether what is contained in those books is true or false, the judgment that it is true lies beyond tests that can be applied by empirical investigation and rational argument. Its truth lies beyond proof, and therefore the judgment that it is true must be an article of faith. The same is to be said about the fundamental belief of Islam; namely, that the prophet Muhammad received the Koran directly from Allah. That lies beyond proof and so, if true, it must be an article of Islamic faith.

The point to be stressed is that if articles of faith, which are unprovable, have truth in the same sense as the testable and provable conclusions of historical research, science, and philosophy, then the fact that they lie beyond proof by empirical evidence and rational argument does not mean that they are exempt from being subject to the logic of truth. When articles of faith are incompatible with one another, both cannot be judged correctly to be true, though both may be false. We may not be able to answer satisfactorily the question of how we can determine which judgment is correct—that one is true and the other false, or that both are false. However, that fact does not in any way alter the situation. Whether or not we can determine in any way, and without any residual doubt, what the correct judgment is, it still remains the case that two incompatible religious beliefs, credal assertions, or articles of faith cannot both be true.

One may object by stating that there are some noncredal religions—that is, religions in which there are no declarative articles of faith that communicants are obliged to affirm. Instead, in such cases it may be said that there are only rules of conduct to be observed, rituals to be performed, or ways of life to be followed. Such religions, it may be thought, have no orthodoxy—no right doctrine or dogmas to be believed. Hence the logic of truth does not apply.

This objection lacks force. Its conclusion is incorrect. There may be religions with no explicit orthodoxy. In such religions, there is an orthopraxy—one right way of living, acting, worshiping, and so on. Such orthopraxy implicitly presupposes an orthodoxy.

The only prescriptive truths that are unquestionable are self-evident ones. It is most unlikely that the rules of conduct and the ritualistic prescriptions of any religion are all self-evidently true. If that is the case, then they must be affirmed as conclusions of reasoning that involves some descriptive propositions about the world or God, propositions that must be judged true even though they cannot be proved.

Thus there is an implicit orthodoxy in the orthopraxy of such religions, and the logic of truth applies to the propositions comprising that implicit orthodoxy in its relation to articles of faith in other religions, credal or noncredal.

In addition, as between two noncredal religions, the prescriptions of one may be incompatible with the prescriptions of the other. The logic of truth is exactly the same for incompatible prescriptive propositions as it is for incompatible descriptive propositions.

(vi)

In the literature devoted to the consideration of truth, there are two quite distinct questions that are often confused. One is the question: What is truth; or what makes a proposition true when it is true? The other is: By what means or criteria can we determine whether this or that proposition is true or false?

The answer to the first question is given by the definition of truth. For all who think reality exists independently of the mind and that reality is what it is regardless of how we think about it, the definition of truth is the agreement of thought with reality. What makes a descriptive proposition true is that it corresponds to the way things really are.

The truth of prescriptive propositions is defined differently, not as conformity with reality but as conformity with right desire. The consequences that follow from this definition of the truth in propositions that contain the words "ought" or "should" need not be developed here, for they do not affect the argument about truth in religion that mainly concerns truth in the articles of faith that constitute orthodoxy in religion. However, readers interested in the consequences, for moral philosophy and ethics in general, of this definition of prescriptive truth will find an account of the matter in Chapter 10 of *Six Great Ideas*.

Only in the context of characteristically modern idealistic philosophies is truth defined in terms other than correspondence with reality. Idealistic philosophers define truth in terms of coherence, the coherence of the elements that are parts in the whole of the mind's realm of thought.[5]

The definition of truth as correspondence or agreement of thought with reality does not immediately yield an answer to the second question. Such correspondence is not immediately and intuitively discernible as is the resemblance between a portrait and the person being portrayed. However, if a true proposition is one that accurately describes the way things really are, then if we act upon it, our action should work successfully. For example, if we think a certain door in a room is the door into another room and not the door to a closet, opening that door should not frustrate our wish to enter the other room. The proposition describing the character of that door is true because it corresponds to the way things are in that room. The success of the action taken on the basis of that proposition enables us to determine the correctness of our judgment that the proposition is true.

This is the pragmatic theory of how to determine whether our judgment about the truth of a proposition is correct or not. As William James developed this so-called pragmatic

---

5. See my discussion of philosophical idealism as an exclusively modern error in *Intellect: Mind Over Matter* (New York, 1990), Chapters 7 and 8.

theory of truth, he recognized that underlying it was the ancient definition of truth as the agreement of thought with reality. He also acknowledged that other tests or criteria entered into the process of determining whether a given proposition was true or false.

It should be provable in a variety of ways. It should be verified and corroborated. It should be assimilable to the body of knowledge we already possess or, if not, then some aspect of that knowledge may have to be changed if the new proposition is to be judged true on the basis of other tests. This last point introduces the criterion of coherence into the pragmatic theory of truth even though James, as a realist, adopted the definition of truth in terms of correspondence with reality.

In the dispute between William James and F. H. Bradley about truth that went on during the first decade of this century, the two disputants never joined issue. James, the realist, answering the first question about truth by employing the definition of it in terms of correspondence with reality, then proceeded to answer the second question by setting forth a variety of tests for determining whether a given proposition is true or false—whether our judgment about its truth is correct or not. Bradley, the idealist, having denied an independent reality, necessarily rejected the definition of truth in terms of correspondence. In developing his coherence theory of truth, he merged the second question with the first.

(vii)

Without adjudicating the dispute between Bradley and James, we can see that coherence is an essential element in the logic of truth whether or not it is the definition of truth or only one test or criterion in the process of determining whether a particular proposition is true or false. Centuries earlier this element of coherence entered into the logic of truth by way of the controversy that took place between Thomas Aquinas and the Latin followers of the Arabic philosopher Averroës. It deals with a point in the logic of truth that is crucial for our consideration of truth in religion.

An Arabic philosopher named Algazeli had written a book entitled *The Destruction of the Philosopher* in which, as a man of Muslim faith, he rejected the main propositions of the Aristotelian philosophy that were incompatible with his faith. Averroës, who had been persuaded of the truth of Aristotelian philosophy, recently introduced into the Muslim West, wrote a reply entitled *The Destruction of the Destruction*. In it he proclaimed that there were two different bodies of truth: on the one hand the truths of faith; on the other hand the truths of reason. These two bodies of truth existed in what might be called "logic-tight compartments." No question arose or had to be confronted about their compatibility or incompatibility—their coherence—with one another.[6]

There was, therefore, no possible conflict between philosophy and religion. Both could peacefully coexist, but unfortunately for the peace of the community, Averroës did not say "coexist side by side," for he definitely assigned a superior status to the truths of reason and an inferior status to the truths of faith—the one belonging to the sphere of intellect, the other to the sphere of the imagination.

In his attack on the Latin Averroists, Aquinas defended the diametrically opposite view. Although his opponents did not

6. See Étienne Gilson, *Reason and Revelation in the Middle Ages* (New York, 1938), pp. 35–58.

publicly state their commitment to a theory of double truth, Aquinas, in his criticism of the Latin Averroists, implicitly accused them of it. He condemned as false the claim that a proposition could be factually true in philosophy or science and at the same time factually false in religious faith. There is only one all-embracing sphere of logical or factual truth, in which all the parts, however various or diverse they may be in other respects, must be coherent and compatible with one another.[7]

If what Averroës had in mind in speaking of the two truths was that, as distinct from the truths of reason, the truths of faith were poetical truths appropriate to narratives, then Aquinas as an Aristotelian might have granted the existence of two truths.

Let it not be thought that to attribute poetical truth to a mythology or a religion degrades its significance for human life. Meaning or significance is not dependent on the logical truth of what is being said or thought. Much can be learned from the poetical truth that resides in works of the imagination. In his *Poetics*, Aristotle maintained that the two functions performed by poetry ("poetry" meaning all the works of fine art, not just dramatic and epic narrations) are to give us instruction and delight. The instruction he had in mind derived from the insights and the understanding that result from the imaginative exploration of the possibilities and probabilities. These certainly enrich one's understanding of the actual, about which we have instruction from history, science, and philosophy.

Aquinas's quarrel with Averroës was not that the latter had

---

7. See Thomas Aquinas, *The Trinity and the Unicity of the Intellect*, trans. R. E. Brennan (St. Louis, 1946).

distinguished between two kinds of truth that could not conflict with one another—logical and poetical truth, truths of reason and truths of the imagination. Being an Aristotelian, Aquinas would not have found that distinction an objectionable innovation. What he objected to was that Averroës had given the truths of religious faith an inferior status and had attributed to them a character that made it impossible for religious beliefs to come into conflict with the conclusions of science and philosophy.

His own view of the matter was that the truths of faith and the truths of reason were exactly the same kind of truth and subject to the same logic, which made it quite possible for one domain to challenge the other. To say that something is logically rather than poetically true is to say it is factually true, that this truth corresponds to the facts of reality, to the way things really are.

For Aquinas, the truths of faith, coming from God, were superior to the truths of reason, but since they were not different kinds of truth, they could come into conflict with one another. Such conflict had to be resolved, because all truths that were logical and factual had to be coherent and compatible with one another in the unity of truth.

Aquinas used the term "Averroist" for those who held views opposed to his on these two points. The term, when used in a disapprobative manner, applies only to those who deny that religious beliefs and scientific or philosophical conclusions have the *same kind* of truth and who deny that they can come into conflict with one another.

When the rabbis in Amsterdam anathematized and excommunicated Benedict Spinoza for what they regarded as atheism in the conception of God set forth in his *Ethics*, they were agreeing with Aquinas that the truths of faith were the same kind of truths as the truths of philosophy. Hence, if the Jewish faith claimed truth for the proposition that God created the universe and also transcended it, the rabbis had to reject as false Spinoza's theory of an uncreated universe in which God is totally immanent.

(viii)

According to the position of Aquinas in his dispute with those whom he called Averroists, truth is one comprehensive, integral, and coherent whole in which there are many parts, each part differing in the methods by which truth is pursued and also in the aspects of reality with which that pursuit is concerned.

Mathematical truth is a part of that whole; so is the truth of all the various empirical sciences; so also is the truth achieved by historical research and by philosophical thought; and, finally, if religious truth is not poetical truth of the kind to be found in myths and other forms of fictional narrative, then it, too, is simply one part in the whole of truth that must have coherence and be compatible with all the other parts of the whole. That, briefly stated, is what is required by the logic of truth in terms of the unity of truth.

One difference between religious truth—the truth of religious creeds, dogmas, or articles of faith—and all the other parts of truth named above is a feature previously noted; namely, that the truths of faith or religious belief are beyond proof by any empirical or rational means. The parts of truth that are most amenable to proof are the truths of mathematics, of empirical science, and of historical research. In relation to these parts of truth, the part that consists of philosophical truth is subject to doubt when it comes into conflict with historical truth or with the truths achieved by the empirical sciences.

With regard to questions that are answerable only by means

of philosophical inquiry and reflection, no conflict can be tolerated between philosophy and the other parts of truth. With regard to such matters, philosophy has its own methods for ascertaining which of several incompatible philosophical doctrines can be correctly judged true. But religion has none of the ordinary means or methods—no appeals to experience or reason—for judging where the truth lies when it affirms, denies, or contradicts what is denied or affirmed by other parts of truth.

This raises the question: How shall such conflicts or incompatibilities be resolved when they occur? The only answer to this question with which I am aquainted (other than the Averroistic answer that puts apparently conflicting truths into logic-tight compartments) is that given by Augustine in his rules for the interpretation of what were for him Sacred Scriptures—the Old and the New Testaments.

It must be remembered that in his young manhood, Augustine read the Scriptures at the behest of his mother. At that time, full of the secular learning of his day, he dismissed the Bible out of hand as consisting of stories fit only for the minds of children as fables and myths are, not for mature minds exercising their critical intelligence. He had read the words in their literal meaning. In consequence of that, a well-educated person, such as he was, could not have done otherwise than to throw the book away. Only later, after he had heard in Milan St. Ambrose deliver a sermon on the text "the letter killeth, the spirit giveth life," did he take up the Holy Scriptures once more and try to go beyond the literal meanings of the words to the moral, allegorical, anagogical, and spiritual meanings to be found in the things literally signified by words of the text.

After his conversion to Christianity in his thirty-third year, Augustine became the formative Father of the early Church, developing the orthodoxy that was initially formulated in the Nicene Creed. He understood that Christian orthodoxy was to be drawn from the Sacred Scriptures as the revealed word of God. He understood that the first article of his Christian faith was that God had revealed Himself to man through the human voices that had been inspired to communicate His message.

Since the Bible is divinely inspired, the message it conveys must be true; but since it conveys that message in human words, which are totally misleading if they are read literally and *only* in that way, St. Augustine realized that the first task of the theologian was that of exegesis, of going beyond the literal meaning of words by various steps and stages of interpretation. Only then could articles of faith be formulated. Only then could the theologian do his work of trying to understand philosophically the dogmas that declared what should be believed.

Augustine acknowledged the existence of the many different interpretations that were extant in his day and that agitated the thought of the early Fathers. While upholding the possibility of multiple interpretations, he was also persuaded that these diverse interpretations might not be equally correct. He, therefore, recommended two rules that should be followed in interpreting Sacred Scriptures.

His first precept was: Hold to the truth of Scripture without wavering. Since it is the revealed truth, we must never abandon our belief in its truth.

His second precept followed: Since Sacred Scriptures can be interpreted in a multiplicity of senses, one should adhere to a particular version only in such measure as to be ready to abandon it if it should prove to be false, lest Holy Scripture be exposed to the ridicule of nonbelievers and obstacles be placed in the way of their believing.

(ix)

It is impossible to exaggerate the profound significance of Augustine's second precept in the light of the logic of truth that we have been considering. How can an interpretation of Sacred Scripture, one that leads to the formulation of an article of faith, be proved to be false? The essence of faith is to be beyond proof. Since Augustine knew all this, as we can tell from his little essay on "The Profit of Believing," what then could he have possibly meant by speaking of articles of faith as being subject to disproof?

It is only by appealing to Aquinas's doctrine of the unity of truth, set forth in his disputation with the Averroists eight hundred years later, that I can solve that puzzle.

Let us, for example, suppose an interpretation of Sacred Scripture that leads to the formulation of an article of faith that is contrary to a truth that has been established beyond a reasonable doubt by scientific investigation or by philosophical reasoning. If Augustine were confronted with what is here being supposed, would he not be able to conclude, in the light of his own two precepts, that the interpretation in this case was incorrect and that no article of faith should be based upon it?

Logically speaking, disproof consists in the proof of a contrary or contradictory proposition. This amounts to a *disproof* of the questionable interpretation and to its rejection as an illegitimate article of faith, which might have been formulated on the basis of it. According to the logic of truth, no interpretation of Sacred Scripture and no article of faith to which it leads can be true if it is incompatible with what is known with certitude in other parts of the whole truth, such as mathematics, science, and philosophy. Understood in this way, Augustine's second precept leads to the logical disproof and rejection of articles of faith that are incompatible with what is known *with certitude* in one or more fields of natural knowledge, such as mathematics, science, and philosophy.

I have laid stress on the words "with certitude" because they introduce a qualification that greatly complicates the picture. There is little in all the fields of our natural knowledge, based upon empirical research and rational reflection, that we know with certitude—little that is beyond the shadow of a doubt. That being the case, there may be very few instances in which we might be called upon to reject an article of faith because of its incompatibility with what we know *with certitude*. Nevertheless, if instead of "certitude" we substitute the weaker standard "beyond a reasonable doubt," there may be many articles of religious faith, not only in Christianity but in most other world religions, that become questionable because of what, at a given time, we claim to know in history, empirical science, and philosophy beyond a reasonable doubt.

It may be useful here to offer an example, in the case of Christianity, of scientific and technological advances that may call an article of faith into question. If the prediction of computer technologists and researchers into artificial intelligence is ever realized—that machines can be constructed in the future, the behavior of which will be indistinguishable from the behavior of human beings—then the Christian belief in the immortality of the human soul will be challenged. That belief depends for its rational support on the immateriality of the human intellect.

If purely material machines can do everything the human intellect can do, in a manner that is indistinguishable from the performance of the intellect, then there is no philosophical ground for affirming the immateriality of the intellect.[8] However, it may still be affirmed as an article of faith, though making that article of faith intelligible becomes more difficult. Unsupported philosophically, the immortality of the soul may become a mystery of faith.

If the claim made by scientists in the field of artificial intelligence could ever be affirmed with certitude, beyond the shadow of a doubt, then the contradictory philosophical proposition (that the intellect is immaterial) would be disproved; and with that, the religious belief in the immortality of the soul might become questionable, or at least difficult to understand. Even if that claim can never be established with certitude, but only beyond a reasonable doubt, the Christian dogma concerning immortality would be seriously challenged and be made subject to grave doubt. What has just been said about a Christian belief, by way of example, applies in exactly the same way to religious beliefs in other religions, especially those beliefs that lie beyond proof by empirical evidence and rational argument. They can in the same way be made subject to serious doubt.

(x)

The crucial and indispensable premise in this line of reasoning is the rejection of Averroism by affirming the unity of truth. In the realm of all truths consisting of propositions that can be affirmed or denied, incompatible truths cannot coexist. All the diverse parts of knowledge, including religious knowledge or knowledge by faith, must coherently form one and only one integral whole.

---

8. On this point, see my recent book *Intellect: Mind Over Matter*, especially Chapter 3.

One more story about Augustine may further illuminate the point that has just been made. In his youth and while he was a teacher of rhetoric, Augustine was greatly attracted by the Manicheanism then prevalent in the Hellenistic world. It appealed to him more than Christianity did. What caused him finally to turn away and reject it were the astrological predictions that were part of Manichean teaching. Learned in the Greek science of his day, the truths of which conflicted with Manichean astrology, Augustine dismissed the Manichean religion as unworthy of belief. It was discredited in his eyes.

Great progress has been made since Augustine's day in all fields of historical research and scientific investigation. Sixteen centuries later, in the time of Cardinal Newman, much more historical and scientific truth could be affirmed beyond a reasonable doubt. When John Henry Newman was wrestling with the problem of converting from the Church of England to Roman Catholicism, he wrote a book entitled *An Essay on the Development of Christian Doctrine* in which he recorded the extraordinary changes that had occurred in the dogmas of the Church since Patristic time. Not only had historical and scientific knowledge expanded greatly since the time of Augustine and the early Fathers of the Church, but so also had the body of religious beliefs that the faithful were called upon to affirm.

However, throughout that long historical development, the relation between faith and reason remained unaltered. No article of faith should remain firm among the dogmas of the Church if what it claims to be true runs counter to what we know by other means and methods. If we know the contrary with certitude, then it should be dismissed or discredited. If we know the contrary beyond a reasonable doubt, it should still be regarded as doubtful even if the doubt may be questionable.

Throughout the preceding discussion I have referred to philosophy as representing one part of the whole truth along with mathematics and empirical science. But we must observe an important difference between philosophy on the one hand, and mathematics and empirical science on the other.

As I have previously stated, mathematics and empirical science are transcultural, as philosophy is not—at least not yet.[9] Wherever twentieth-century technology is employed, the mathematical and scientific truths that underlie it are either explicitly or implicitly affirmed. No matter how they differ in all other cultural respects—in their religions, their philosophies, their interpretation of history, and their mythologies —all cultural communities on this globe that use the technological devices now available affirm, at least implicitly, the mathematics and the natural sciences on which technology is based.

When, in the chapters to follow, we come to deal with the great religions of the Far East, we cannot use our knowledge of history and philosophy in testing the truth of various Far Eastern religious beliefs. These two subjects are not yet transcultural. But because of the global spread of twentieth-century technology, mathematics and empirical natural science have become transcultural. Therefore, they can play the role that Augustine had in mind when he enjoined Christians to use what they know by other means to check what is proposed for their belief in the realm of faith.

As I pointed out in Chapter 1, philosophy, in my conception of it, should become transcultural. It can do so by passing Augustine's test of truth with regard to interpretations of Holy Scripture. An interpretation cannot be true or is seriously doubtful if it conflicts with what, at a given time, we know

---

9. What is here said of philosophy can also be said of the interpretations that historical narratives contain; less so the factual conclusions of historical research.

through science either beyond the shadow of a doubt or beyond a reasonable doubt.

The same test applies to the principles and conclusions of philosophical thought. Claiming logical truth, they can be contradicted by what, at a given time, is established scientific knowledge. If a philosophical doctrine passes this test, then there is no reason why it should not be as transcultural as is the scientific knowledge with which it is compatible.[10]

(xi)

Most of the great religions of the world, both those of Western and those of Far Eastern origin, affirm the existence of a spiritual being or, at least, a spiritual aspect or dimension of reality. It may be thought that such religious beliefs (as, for example, the belief in angels and in God as purely spiritual beings) come directly into conflict with the knowledge we have of the material cosmos through the physical sciences. But that is not the case.

The conflict is not with our scientific knowledge of the physical world but with the dogmatic materialism of a great many scientists and with the materialistic monism that has been more frequently asserted in modern philosophy. That assertion should be dismissed as sheer dogmatism. Angels, for example, may not exist, but their existence is not impossible.

---

10. Two philosophical doctrines may, of course, be incompatible with one another so that both cannot be true even if both pass the test of not being incompatible with established scientific knowledge. In that case, the question of where the truth lies, as between these incompatible philosophical doctrines, must be resolved by philosophical analysis and argument.

No proof can be given for the proposition that nothing exists except bodies, corporeal entities, or material things. Only the proof of that proposition would make the existence of angels impossible or make impossible the existence of spiritual aspects of reality.[11]

I must add a point I shall explain more fully later. This injunction is applicable to the religions and cultures of the Far East only if they come to accept the logic of truth and its controlling insight about the unity of truth; in short, Western logic.

I know that I risk being charged with Western parochialism or provincialism in the foregoing statement. Nevertheless, I feel obliged to take that risk because, in my view, the fundamentals of logic should be as transcultural as the mathematics with which the principles of logic are associated. The principles of logic are neither Western nor Eastern, but universal.

(xii)

So far I have dealt only with the logical disproof of religious beliefs—articles of faith that cannot be proved but can be disproved by the proof of propositions that are their logical contraries or contradictories.

There are certain limits to logical disproof. An affirmative existential proposition can be proved, but a negative existential proposition—one that denies the existence of some thing—cannot be proved.

---

11. For further discussion of this point, see my book *The Angels and Us* (New York, 1982), pp. 103–107.

Here lies the weakness of all attempts by philosophical atheists to prove that God does not exist. Though the philosophical arguments for the existence of God may fall short of certitude, offering reasons that support an affirmative conclusion only beyond a reasonable doubt, the philosophical atheist has never been able to construct a logically valid argument that supports the opposite conclusion and thus constitutes a disproof of God's existence.

What, then, can the atheist do? He can offer rhetorical, rather than logical, arguments, arguments that aim to weaken the religious belief in God—in effect, to discredit it, which means to render it less credible. By asking in a variety of ways how, with all the manifest evil in the world, anyone can believe in an infinitely good creator, the atheist poses a problem for the believer that is difficult to answer. Astute theologians can answer that question, but not ordinary persons of religious faith. Insinuating that question into their minds may not only be troubling to them, it may also have an insidious undercutting effect on the firmness of their belief.

There are many different ways in which, by discrediting them rather than disproving them, religious beliefs can be attacked rhetorically. One way is in the manner of Voltaire. He attacked a proposition in the theodicy of the German philosopher Gottfried Leibniz, the proposition that God being perfectly good, the cosmos he created must be the best of all possible worlds.

Aquinas earlier advanced good reasons for denying that this was the best of all possible worlds. Voltaire, unacquainted with Aquinas on this point, does not argue against that proposition. In his *Candide*, he simply ridicules Dr. Pangloss, whom he presents as a disciple of Leibniz, and makes him a laughingstock by having him repeat, after each disaster that Candide encounters, the solemn statement that, after all, this is the best of all possible worlds.

Another example of rhetorical attack on religious belief is the "higher criticism" of the Bible by Ernest Renan in the nineteenth century. By questioning the historical authenticity of biblical texts, Renan did not logically disprove the articles of Christian faith that had their basis in Sacred Scripture and were accepted as divinely revealed. But Renan's work and that of his followers did have a discrediting effect on religious belief that relied too simply on a literal and unsophisticated reading of the Bible.

In our own day, the work of Professor Joseph Campbell in comparative mythology represents still another mode of rhetorical attack on religious belief, aiming to discredit, not disprove, beliefs for which their adherents claim factual truth.

For example, his book entitled *The Hero with a Thousand Faces* tells its readers that in the mythologies of many human tribes there are Christ-like figures who resemble the historical Jesus whom Christians believe to be the incarnation of God come to earth for the redemption and salvation of the human race.

This hardly proves that Christian faith in Christ as the second person of the Trinity, the son of God who died on the cross for mankind's salvation, is historically and factually false. Yet by recounting tribal myths that have some resemblance to the Christian belief, Campbell clearly aims to discredit that belief, to cast doubt upon it, to render it less credible.

What these many similar myths make manifest is something common to the human race as a whole: mankind's sense of its delinquency and the inadequacy of its own powers to raise itself up from its earthly condition, its need for help from above to rise above where it finds itself. This fact about a feeling common to many human groups at many times and places has no logical bearing whatsoever on the factual truth or falsity of the scriptural accounts of the historical Jesus of

Nazareth or upon the Christian beliefs that are derived from those accounts.

In the next chapter I shall return to Joseph Campbell's reduction of all of the world's religions to mythologies that may have poetical truth but, in his view, certainly do not have any logical or factual truth. They are, in his terms, misconstrued mythologies, incorrectly adopted by one religion or another as if they had factual truth.

The evidence Campbell advances for this view of religion consists entirely in the many similarities between stories and figures in mythologies that are not established institutional religions in today's world with stories and figures to be found in the established religions. Such evidence has only rhetorical force in discrediting religious beliefs; it has no logical force whatsoever in disproving them.

Valid logical arguments that constitute proofs or disproofs are intellectually convincing. Rhetorical arguments, if effective, are persuasive, emotionally or intellectually, but never convincing.

CHAPTER 3

The Study of Religion and Mythology

(i)

Until the nineteenth century, religion was not a subject of academic study or research. If there were teachers and students of religion, they did their teaching and studying in the great universities of the Middle Ages, in the parochial schools of Christian and Muslim countries, and in the Yeshiva schools of Hassidic Jewish communities.

If the subject matter of such teaching went beyond the catechism in Christian lands or its analogues in Muslim countries and Jewish communities, it usually dwelt on the institutional history of the religion with which it was concerned. If it became at all philosophical and ventured into the difficult territory that is concerned with religious truth, it took the form of apologetics or dogmatic theology.

Apologetics is the effort on the part of a person of a given religious faith to argue for its exclusive or superior possession of the truth as against all other competing faiths. From the point of view of the apologist's own faith, those with differing beliefs are usually called infidels.

A very good example of Christian apologetics is to be found in the *Pensées* of Blaise Pascal, who, we should remember, was a great mathematician and physicist. Not all of his *Pensées* is devoted to Christian apologetics, but a considerable portion of it is; Sections VIII–XIII are, especially Section IX, in which he discusses Christianity in relation to Judaism and Islam.[12]

A treatise by Boethius entitled *On the Catholic Faith* provides us with an example of apologetics from antiquity; and Cardinal Newman's *Grammar of Assent* is an example from the nineteenth century. A seventeenth-century work by John Locke might also be cited as an example of Christian apologetics: *The Reasonableness of Christianity*. There are similarities between Locke's argument here and the views of Augustine and Aquinas concerning the coherence and compatibility of the truths of faith with the truths of reason.

Dogmatic theology differs from apologetics in that its aim is not to argue for or defend the truth of a particular religion, but rather to employ philosophical analysis and reasoning to render the dogmas of that religion's creed intelligible, as far as that is possible with the mysteries of faith; and beyond that, in the moral part of dogmatic theology, to render intelligible the precepts of the divine law and the institution of the sacraments.

Dogmatic theology, thus described, flourished in the Middle Ages, along with scholastic philosophy, in Muslim and Jewish religious communities as well as in the great universities of

---

12. While apologetics does not play a large part in the writings of Augustine, certain passages bear on the relation of Christianity to other religions in antiquity. See *The City of God*, Book XIX, Chapters 22–23; and *On Christian Doctrine*, Book II, Chapters 40–42. There is even less apologetical content in the *Summa Theologica* of Thomas Aquinas, but see therein his *Treatise on Faith*, in Part II-II, Question 10.

Christian Europe; and it has remained a university subject until the present day in Muslim, Jewish, and Christian institutions of higher learning.

In the twentieth century, for the first time, a study of religion that was not parochial and neither apologetical nor theological came into being. In most of our colleges and universities this study is either described as the history of religions and religious institutions or as the comparative study of the differing world religions. Its emergence as an academic innovation coincided with the emergence of cultural anthropology and comparative sociology. An early work that can be taken as representative of this new departure was Max Weber's book *The Sociology of Religion*. J. G. Frazer's *The Golden Bough* is another early representative of this approach to the subject, in which the line that divides religion from mythology is shadowy.

What characterizes this sociological approach to the study of religion, and especially the plurality of religions, is that, with few exceptions, the scientific and historical students of religion are themselves not persons of any religious faith and are not participating communicants in any religious community. They are seldom, if ever, concerned with questions about the truth to be found in religions—the kind of truth that differs in only one respect from the truth to be found in history, empirical science, and philosophy; namely, that it cannot be proved, though, as we have seen, it can be disproved by its incompatibility with what is otherwise judged to be true.

Let me summarize. An apologetical approach to the study of religion is concerned with defending the truth of one religion against the claims of others, which it rejects as false. The approach of dogmatic theology to the study of religion is concerned with rendering as intelligible as possible the dogmatically declared articles of faith believed to be true by the communicants of that religion, but not in defending them. The study of religion by historians and social scientists is concerned with what the various world religions under comparison say, but not with which of them, if any, is true. In the light of this summary, a philosophical approach provides the only study of religion that considers all religions impartially, while at the same time it holds them all to the standard of truth, so that alone it can be said to deal with the difficult problems raised by the plurality of religions and the unity of truth.

(ii)

The philosophy of religion, like the history, sociology, and psychology of it, is a relatively recent academic innovation. It certainly did not exist in antiquity and the Middle Ages. Both David Hume and Immanuel Kant wrote philosophical treatises about what they called "natural religion," something quite distinct from Christianity, which they regarded as having, or as claiming to have, a supernatural foundation.[13] Georg Hegel, Friedrich Schleiermacher, and other German philosophers lectured on the philosophy of religion, but I cannot find in their works a solution to the problem with which we are here concerned.[14]

A philosophy of religion, it seems to me, should try to find answers to five main questions: (1) How shall religion be defined so that when the word "religion" is used univocally

---

13. Hume wrote *Dialogues Concerning Natural Religion*; Kant, *Religion Within the Limits of Reason Alone.*

14. Hegel's work is entitled *Lectures on the Philosophy of Religion*; and Schleiermacher's, *On Religion: Speeches to Its Cultured Despisers.* For Schleiermacher, religion was based on intuition and feeling and was independent of all dogma. Its highest experience was a sense of union with the infinite. Hegel strongly opposed this view of religion.

as defined (i.e., in exactly the same sense), it applies to all the well-known religions of the present world and to nothing else? (2) How should the various world religions be classified? What are the differing main types of religion? (3) How should the line be drawn between mythology and religion? (4) How should the line be drawn between philosophy and religion? (5) What can be said about truth in religion when conflicting religious beliefs are considered in relation to one another and also in relation to what is judged to be true in history, empirical science, and philosophy?

Reserving my attempt to answer questions four and five until the concluding chapter of this book, I will try to present brief answers to the other three. But before I do that, let me say at once that a philosopher of religion, unlike a religious apologist or a dogmatic theologian, should write from the point of view of no particular religious faith. What is proper for a religious apologist and a dogmatic theologian is not proper for a philosopher of religion. This would appear to throw the philosopher of religion into the same camp with historians and social scientists who also proceed without the benefit of one or another religious faith.

That, however, need not be the case. Unlike the history of religions and the sociological examination of diverse religious institutions, the philosophy of religion should be, above all, concerned with the problem of truth in religion, with that concern illuminated by an understanding of the logic of truth and of its unity.[15] Very few of the books that claim to be

---

15. The psychological approach to religion (as, for example, in *The Varieties of Religious Experience* by William James) is not concerned with the truth in religious doctrines or in articles of religious faith. It is concerned rather with the psychological effects of religious belief on individuals, regardless of whether the beliefs are true or false. For Karl Marx, religious belief is the opiate of the masses. Its psychological influence is something quite apart from its truth or falsity.

philosophies of religion discharge that obligation. Further-more, few, if any, of them consider the great religions of Far Eastern origin.

This is of the utmost importance to remember when we come to the problem of the plurality of religions and the unity of truth. It is here that the philosopher of religion, even if he is also a person of religious faith, must proceed without at-tributing truth to one religion rather than another. If he has no faith, that is not difficult to do. If he has faith, he must hold it in abeyance in order to proceed as a philosopher.

(iii)

The definition of religion. In the large array of things for which the word "religion" is used, only some are organized and institutionalized forms of human conduct and belief that involve communities so constituted that an individual is either a member of it or an outsider, and the membership of the community consists of a fairly large population. It is in this sense of the word that there are in existence today a plurality of world religions; and it is only in this sense of the word that we are concerned with truth in religion.

Without attempting to give an exhaustive enumeration of the properties or characteristics that help us to identify the various religions, which differ from one another in so many respects, here are the traits that are common to all or to most.

Some form of worship is present in all religions. The form of worship differs from one religion to another in its specific rituals, ceremonials, and sacrifices. In all religions, the reli-gious practices involve a separation of the sacred or holy from the secular and the profane: there are sacred places, sacred objects, sacred animals, sacred words, sacred prayers, and so forth.

The institutions of organized religion, with the exception of the Quakers, also include a separation of a priesthood from a laity, though the words used to name these two groups differ from religion to religion. Only one of these two groups of persons has the authority to perform certain ceremonies or rituals, which are more or less necessary to worship. In this group of authorized religious officials, there is usually a hierarchy of offices having different responsibilities in the church, temple, synagogue, mosque, synod, or holy place, whatever its name may be.

In all religions there is something like a code of religious laws, precepts, or prescriptions that outline, in varying degrees of detail, a way of life or a style of conduct to be followed by those who seek salvation, conceived as the attainment of a spiritual goal, never as one or another form of worldly success.

This body of precepts may include the prescriptions of moral philosophy or what some philosophers call the precepts of the natural moral law, but it always goes beyond that to include mandates that have no basis in ordinary morality.

Finally, a religion, as defined, obliges its communicants or the members of its community to affirm as true a set of explicitly stated beliefs that constitute its dogmatically declared creed; or, as indicated earlier, its orthodoxy may not be explicitly declared but it is implicit in and presupposed by the code of conduct that a religion prescribes for its members. In either case, there are religious beliefs that involve affirmations and denials, about which the question of truth must be raised.

(iv)

The classification of religions: the major kinds into which they are divided. I shall proceed in terms of the definition of organized, institutionalized religion given above. Let the first division be between religions that are explicitly credal, religions that have dogmatically declared articles of faith, on the one hand; and, on the other hand, those religions that are explicitly preceptorial and legalistic. The latter are credal only in the affirmative or negative beliefs about matters of fact that their precepts, prescriptions, or rules of conduct presuppose. It is obviously easier to deal with the problem of truth in the explicitly credal religions. Nevertheless, and however difficult it may be to explicate the implicit, presupposed beliefs, the problem remains the same.

Among the credal religions, the main division is between articles of faith that include the affirmation of one or more supernatural deities on the one hand; and, on the other hand, articles of faith that do not affirm the existence of one or more supernatural beings but instead affirm characteristics of the cosmos, usually spiritual characteristics, that are not known to the empirical natural sciences and lie beyond the reach of philosophical insight and analysis (i.e., they are not accessible to the methods of inquiry available in these disciplines).

The first group of religions can be called theological; the second, cosmological. The theological religions divide into the monotheistic and the polytheistic. A religion is monotheistic even if the godhead involves a plurality of persons, as does the Christian trinity. A religion is polytheistic if its several deities are existentially distinct, even if one deity is regarded as supreme. By this criterion, no religion can be both monotheistic

47

and polytheistic. Where religions are polytheistic, there may be a hierarchy of gods and a difference between gods and demi-gods, but the supremacy of one god among many is not equivalent to the affirmation of the God that is the one and only supreme being.

The cosmological religions cannot be so easily subdivided. Perhaps the only difference that is clear here is that between (1) cosmological religions that affirm the existence of a spiritual reality over and above the physical universe in which we live, and (2) cosmological religions that affirm spiritual aspects of nature that are undetectable by natural science.

(v)

The first division in the classification of religions is made by the line that separates the explicitly credal religions from all the rest, which are instead explicitly preceptorial religions. These religions, however, are implicitly credal by virtue of the descriptive articles of faith that their laws, rules of conduct, rituals, and ceremonies presuppose.

Judaism, Christianity, Islam, Buddhism, and Taoism are clear examples of credal religions that have explicit orthodoxies as well as explicit orthopraxies. Among the living religions in the world today, Hinduism, Jainism, Sikhism, Confucianism, and Shintoism are examples of preceptorial religions. They have explicit orthopraxies but no explicit orthodoxies.

The second division draws a line between religions that are theological and religions that are cosmological. Among the above credal religions, only Buddhism and Taoism are cosmological—religions without belief in one or more deities. Among the above explicitly preceptorial (and only implicitly credal) religions, it is difficult to determine the extent to which Confucianism is theological and the extent to which it is cosmological.

Among the theological religions, only Judaism, Christianity, and Islam are explicitly monotheistic. Hinduism is polytheistic, as is Shintoism. Among the cosmological religions, Buddhism is a religion that affirms the existence of a spiritual reality over and above the world of physical nature; and Taoism is a religion that affirms spiritual aspects of nature not detectable by the natural sciences.

The line that divides religion and mythology is most shadowy in the case of Hinduism, though there is mythological content in many of the world's great religions. Confucianism and Taoism probably have the least.

Finally, the line that divides religion from philosophy—drawn between religions that claim to have their basis in divine revelation and religions that make no such claim—separates the three great religions of Western origin from almost all of the great religions of Far Eastern origin, with the possible exception of Buddhism, which claims a basis in an illumination experienced by Buddha.[16] (See the accompanying table that summarizes the classification of the major world religions.)

In all of the above kinds of religion, the explicitly declared creeds or articles of faith share one common characteristic. In every case, the beliefs carry with them claims to truth, the correctness of which cannot be determined by the means em-

---

16. I am indebted to Wendy Doniger O'Flaherty, Mircea Eliade Professor of the History of Religions at the University of Chicago, for assistance in naming religions that exemplify the categories in my classification of religions. The terms of that classification are mine, not hers. Any mistakes I have made in placing extant religions in one category or another are also mine, not hers.

PRINCIPAL DISTINCTIONS AMONG THE WORLD'S RELIGIONS

	I		II			III	IV
	Credal	Preceptorial	Theological Mono.	Poly.	Cosmological	Amount of Mythology	Revelation
Buddhism	X				X	Minimal	?
Christianity	X		X			Minimal	YES
Confucianism		X		X		Minimal	NO
Hinduism		X		X		Large	NO
Islam	X		X			Minimal	YES
Jainism		X			X	Large	NO
Judaism	X	X	X			Minimal	YES
Shinto		X		X		Large	NO
Sikhism		X	X			Minimal	NO
Taoism	X				X	Minimal	NO

ployed for testing the correctness of historical, scientific, or philosophical judgments about the truth of propositions in their respective fields of inquiry. However, claims of religions to truth can be discredited by their incompatibility with transcultural truths affirmed, at a given time, in the empirical natural sciences.

(vi)

Finally, we come to a subdivision that can be made only in the light of a line drawn between human knowledge that is natural and human knowledge that is supernatural. Our knowledge is natural knowledge if the only means involved in attaining it are the powers inherent in the nature of the human mind, which is the same the world over, as is specific human nature.

All the differences observed by cultural anthropologists in the behavioral and intellectual traits of individuals living in different cultures are superficial and acquired, underlying which are the basic common traits that are inherent in human nature. Human beings everywhere have the same sensitive and intellectual powers. When nothing but these are exercised in the acquisition of knowledge, the knowledge is natural.

In sharp contrast, human knowledge is supernatural if human beings come into possession of it only by the gift of it to them by supernatural agencies—by God and his angels or by divinely inspired scripture; by a direct communication from God to a human being; or to human beings from one or more of the deities in a polytheistic pantheon. Supernatural knowledge is knowledge human beings would not possess without divine intervention.

Not all the theological religions make such claims. Obviously, none of the cosmological religions can make such claims. This raises a difficult question that I shall postpone answering for a moment. How do those religions that do not claim supernatural sources and supernatural knowledge draw the line between religion and philosophy with regard to truth in the creeds that they explicitly declare, or the beliefs that are implicitly presupposed by their rules of conduct? I will return to this question in the following section.

(vii)

Mythology and religion. Our everyday use of the word "myth" has a connotation that includes untruth. We ordinarily dismiss certain persuasively contrived stories or accounts as myths when we judge them as simply untrue—not accurate and testable accounts of what happened in the past. The line that divides history from myth is the same as the line that divides fact from fiction. We speak of historical narratives as accurate or say they are correct. We never say that a story is mythologically inaccurate or incorrect.

To say something is a myth is to say that it is fictional rather than factual. It is a made-up story told, perhaps, for some significant purpose, but it is a piece of fiction nevertheless. We think of the stories schoolchildren are told about George Washington and the cherry tree and about Isaac Newton and the falling apple as myths—pleasant fictions or legends but not historical truths.

When we pass from the sphere of the ordinary discourse in which we engage with one another to the academic fields in which historians, sociologists, and cultural anthropologists study the great mythologies of the world, we move into an area in which nonreligious social scientists either find no line or only a very shadowy line between mythology and religion. They admit that not all the myths they have studied have religious significance or are somehow included among the things believed by one religious community or another. But since as scientists or historians they are not concerned with the truth of religious beliefs, they also tend to identify religions with mythologies—mythologies in which this or that group of people still believe.

The communicants of any religion that claims truth for its beliefs would be deeply offended by the reduction of their religion to a mythology. They would interpret that as dismissing their truth-claims as bogus and their beliefs as superstitious.

No one alive today believes in the gods of Olympus or their counterparts in the Roman pantheon. We teach Greek and Roman mythology to schoolchildren, sometimes with the comment that what we now call mythologies were, in antiquity, part of organized, institutionalized, polytheistic religions. The same can be said for the Germanic, Norse, and Icelandic mythologies that once were part of religions that no longer exist.

This reference to Greek mythology reminds us of the second book of Plato's *Republic*, in which he throws the poets out of the ideal state he is attempting to construct. He charges them with telling lies about the gods. When we carefully examine the charge, are we not led to correct it? The poets, such as Homer and Hesiod, told stories about the gods, good stories that certainly had poetical truth. Fictional narratives cannot tell lies if by "lies" we mean intentional misrepresentations of matters of fact.

What bothered Plato was not the mythic character of the

53

stories the poets told about the gods, but rather the fact that the people of ancient Greece were inclined to believe the myths as if they were factually true. If they did that they would be seriously deceived. Plato wanted to protect the citizens of his ideal state from suffering such deception. But that was not the fault of the poets. The fault lay with the prevalent human tendency to believe as factually true the myths or mythologies that should never be regarded or accepted in that way.

Plato himself, as we know from the tenth book of *The Laws*, did not believe in the Olympian gods. In that book, he tried to prove the existence of God, a single divinity utterly different from the pantheon of deities in Greek mythology. So we know that, for him, mythology had no factual truth. His exclusion of the poets from the republic was motivated by his concern with the popular tendency to accept a poetically contrived mythology as factually true.

(viii)

If myths are fictional stories and not factual histories, how do they differ from poetry—that is, narrative literature in the form of novels and dramas? The answer given by Professor Wendy Doniger O'Flaherty in her book *Other Peoples' Myths* is that a poem carries with it the name of its author (the person who made up the story), whereas a myth is a story that does not have a particular person as author. It is a story told over and over again from time immemorial by the people of an ethnic community and cherished by them because of its significance for them, religious or otherwise. Professor O'Flaherty says that she does not see "how to apply 'true' and 'false' to myths"—that is, she does not see how the words "true" and "false" in their strict logical sense can be applied to myths. When people speak of myths as being true, she thinks that they are only commenting on the importance or significance of the myth to them.[17]

Professor O'Flaherty dismisses the myths made up by Plato in his dialogues. They are not myths in her sense of the term. But Plato's myths do throw some light on the kind of truth that may be attributed to myths. When in the *Timaeus* Plato has recourse to the myth of the Demi-urge to give an account of the formation of the cosmos, he calls it "a likely story." If it were offered as a factually true scientific account of the world's origin and formation, it would exclude other accounts, as Plato's myth does not.

Plato's characterization of his myth as a likely story fits Aristotle's definition of poetical truth, about which he says two things. First, he says that poetical truth consists in a narrative about what could have *possibly* happened and even might *probably* happen, but never did *actually* happen. History, as distinct from poetry, narrates what actually happened in the past, so far as we can tell.

Second, he says that poetical truth is more like philosophical or scientific truth than it is like historical truth, because the stories told in poetical narration have a generality not to be found in the historic narration of singular past events.[18]

If we attribute only poetical truth to the great myths with

---

17. Wendy Doniger O'Flaherty, *Other Peoples' Myths* (New York, 1988). If the title of Professor O'Flaherty's book had stressed the word "other," its connotation would have been that other people's religions are mythologies in which they believe, but that one's own religion may not also be regarded as a misconstrued mythology.

18. See the note on Aristotle appended at the end of this chapter.

which Professor O'Flaherty's book deals, then we are also maintaining that they are neither true nor false in the logical sense of these two terms—the sense in which they are used in the realm of mathematics, empirical science, and philosophy. Diverse novels and plays that tell quite different stories do not conflict with one another. They can all have poetical truth in varying degrees. So, too, diverse mythologies can all have poetical truth in varying degrees.

Professor O'Flaherty uses the word "truth" in senses that I cannot identify as either logical or poetical truth. Her definition of a myth is "a story that is sacred to and shared by a group of people who find their most important meanings in it; it is a story believed to have been composed in the past about an event in the past, or, more rarely, in the future, an event that continues to have meaning in the present because it is remembered; it is a story that is part of a larger group of stories."[19]

Several pages later she says that "the best short definition of a myth is that it is a *true story*. But this statement must be immediately qualified: it is regarded as true not literally, but in its implicit meanings."[20] A story that is true literally or factually is a history or part of a historical narrative. That truth is logical truth, not poetical. But what Professor O'Flaherty means by true "in its implicit meanings," I do not understand.

A few lines farther on she writes: "Myths are perceived as true when the reality to which they point has 'always' been perceived as true or becomes newly perceived as true." Here Professor O'Flaherty departs even further from the logical sense

19. O'Flaherty, *Other Peoples' Myths*, p. 27.
20. Ibid., p. 31.

of the word "true." A statement that is true corresponds with reality, but the reality with which it corresponds is not thereby perceived as true.

A few pages farther we find her asking: "When people assert that myths are true, do they say anything more than 'Myths are about important things'?" She then adds: " 'true' and 'false' are woefully inadequate words to apply to myths."[21] Much later in her book, Professor O'Flaherty talks about "contradictory myths, myths that present two contradictory responses to the same basic question."[22]

According to the logic of truth, contradictions occur between two descriptive or two prescriptive statements, when both of them cannot be false and both of them cannot be true. It never occurs between two imaginative stories that, as differing, can both have poetical truth. I do not understand the sense in which Professor O'Flaherty refers to contradictory myths, since she is plainly not using the word "truth" in either its logical or poetical sense.

Increasing my puzzlement is a statement by Professor O'Flaherty on the same page, to the effect that "I don't believe that there is only one true answer to any great human question." If the question is a question in historical research, in science, or in philosophy, I would say exactly the opposite. Hence I must conclude that the logic of truth as I understand it does not apply to any of the senses in which she uses the word "true."

21. Ibid., p. 32.
22. Ibid., p. 145.

(ix)

To write about myths and mythologies as Professor O'Flaherty does leaves the problem of truth in religion almost untouched. Professor Joseph Campbell, however, goes much further in his book *The Inner Reaches of Outer Space*, subtitled *Metaphor as Myth and as Religion*.[23]

Campbell identifies religions with mythologies that are incorrectly believed to be true. The faithful members of any one religious community, subscribing to its own orthodoxy, dismiss other religions as having no truth because they are regarded by them as other peoples' mythologies. In Campbell's view, they are correct in that view of other peoples' religion, as compared with their own. Since in his terms *all* religions are "misunderstood mythologies," they are incorrect in the view that they hold of their own religion, which they misunderstand in exactly the same way. Those whose belief in myths consists in regarding them as factually true historical accounts are confessing their superstitions, not their religious faith.[24]

The misunderstanding, according to Campbell, consists in "the interpretation of mythic metaphors as references to hard fact: the Virgin Birth, for example, as a biological anomaly, or the Promised Land as a portion of the Near East to be claimed and settled by a people chosen of God, the term 'God' here to be understood as denoting an actual, though invisible, masculine personality, who created the universe and is now

---

23. Joseph Campbell, *The Inner Reaches of Outer Space: Metaphor as Myth and as Religion* (New York, 1986).

24. It is worth noting that Campbell's attack on religions as "misunderstood mythologies" is akin to Plato's real reason for throwing the poets out of the Republic.

resident in an invisible, though actual, heaven to which the 'justified' will go when they die, there to be joined at the end of time by their resurrected bodies," to which Campbell adds the question: "What, in the name of Reason or Truth, is a modern mind to make of such evident nonsense?"[25]

Campbell's reference to God as masculine, to the resurrection of the body as if that resurrection were physical not spiritual, to heaven as an actual though invisible *place*, and so on, reveals his lack of understanding of Jewish and Christian theology. In all three of the great religions of Western origin, God is conceived as a purely spiritual being. Not having a body, God cannot have gender. The conception of God as a person is not anthropomorphic. Angels are also conceived as persons, and man as having the lowest degree of personality; yet Campbell uses the word "personal" as if it had anthropomorphic connotations.

---

25. Campbell, *The Inner Reaches of Outer Space*, p. 55; see also pp. 21, 28, 43, 57, 58, 59–61, 99–100, 111–12, 115. These pages contain other statements to the same effect; namely, that no modern mind, instructed by the natural sciences, and especially by the social sciences, could possibly give any credence to the religious beliefs of Orthodox Jews or to the articles of Christian faith summarized in the Nicene Creed. *A fortiori*, Campbell would say the same thing about the faith of Islam, as well as about the beliefs held by all the great religions of Far Eastern origin. If Campbell's TV conversations with Bill Moyers, subsequently published under the title *The Power of Myth* (New York, 1988), had been as explicit on these points as he is in *The Inner Reaches of Outer Space*, he would have offended a great many of the viewers of that TV series and readers of *The Power of Myth*. I recommend to viewers of the Campbell-Moyers TV series that they read an account of Professor Campbell's mental and moral character by Brendan Gill, a friend and colleague of his, that appeared in *The New York Review of Books*, September 28, 1989, pp. 16–19. It reveals serious deficiencies in Campbell's ethical and political views, especially his use of the word "bliss" for a purely psychological state of contentment experienced by anyone who manages to get what he or she individually wants. This notion of bliss is quite contrary to the ancient ethical conception of happiness as a morally good life as a whole, attainable only by moral virtue and the blessings of good fortune.

As for heaven, Campbell obviously is not cognizant of Augustine's interpretation of the opening words of Genesis: "In the beginning God created heaven and earth." According to Augustine, the word "heaven" in this statement does not mean a physical place of any kind whatsoever, but the realm of purely spiritual creatures as opposed to "earth," the domain of corporeal or material things. Heaven is an invisible realm, not a place, in which God and the angels have their existence.[26]

Professor Campbell was undoubtedly a very good social scientist in the field of cultural anthropology. But his competence in dealing with philosophical matters, especially in the field of philosophical theology, is highly questionable. His judgment in this area reflects the dogmatic materialism that is so prevalent in contemporary science, especially in the behavioral sciences. Monistic materialism is dogmatic precisely because it is as unprovable as any article of religious faith.

(x)

Let us return to the question Professor Campbell asked, which led to the foregoing digression: "What, in the name of Reason or Truth, is a modern mind to make of such evident nonsense?" such as the Virgin Birth, the Promised Land, or a masculine God. It is the answer to that question with which we are concerned. In the name of reason and in accordance with the

---

26. Professor Campbell writes as if he were abysmally ignorant of the best in Christian theology or as intentionally inattentive to it. The passage quoted a page or so earlier is a fundamentalist caricature of Christian theology concocted by the mistaken literal interpretation of the Scriptures to which fundamentalists are given.

logic of truth, the answer is well known to most students of social science in their treatment of the world's religions. It is the answer Campbell himself gives in his book. It is as follows: None of the world's organized and institutionalized religions, especially those that are explicitly credal, is *anything but* a mythology, and none has either truth or falsity in the logical sense of these terms. Each, as Santayana said many years ago, is the poetry in which a certain group of people believe. They are in error only if their belief or faith attributes logical and factual truth, rather than merely poetical truth, to the mythology that is the substance of their religion.

Those with religious faith who think their own religion is not a mythology, as other peoples' religions are, make the mistake of thinking that their beliefs have logical truth. Asserted as facts rather than as fictions, *all* religious beliefs are, in logical terms, false. To be more precise, the judgment asserting as true any religious belief about matters of fact is *incorrect*.

Those who concur in Campbell's view of religion—and there are many in the general public as well as in our universities who share his characteristically twentieth-century applause of unrestricted pluralism in mythologies and religion—can have no interest in further steps to solve the problem raised by the plurality of religions and the unity of truth. They already have the answer to the question whether there is truth (logical, not poetical, truth) in any religion. The answer is completely negative.

That negative assertion is dogmatically declared, for it is asserted without proof, as in the case with all dogmatic declarations. "Dogmatics" as Karl Barth used the term, is characteristic of and proper to all articles of religious faith; nothing but "dogmatic" declarations are possible with regard to religious beliefs that are totally beyond proof.

But dogmatism is inexcusably out of place in the sphere of science where logically rigorous proofs, with varying degrees of probative force, are possible and are to be expected. Arguments that have logically probative force are to be found in the exact sciences, but they are seldom discernible in the literature of the social sciences, including cultural anthropology.

Professor Campbell offers no scientific proof of his unqualified generalization that *all* religions are mythologies in disguise. That generalization is not, in any degree, proved by the kind of evidence on which I commented in Section xii of Chapter 2. The evidence offered has only rhetorical force and no probative force whatsoever.

Campbell's unqualified generalization is espoused by many of his colleagues in sociology and cultural anthropology. If it were proved true, that would constitute a logically sound disproof of the claim made by any religion that its beliefs are factually true; and we would have to accept the conclusion that all religious belief asserting matters of fact are false.

The Campbell generalization, however, unproved by the kind of evidence offered and therefore asserted dogmatically, can have only a rhetorical force that does not affect the persons against whom it is directed. It may give emotional comfort to those who are already irreligious and find pleasure in what they regard as confirmation of their disbelief. It may strengthen the doubts of those who already tend to be skeptical about truth in religion. But lacking logically probative force, it will certainly not convince persons of religious faith that what they believe is only myth.

It still remains to be said that the unproved generalization may be true. It must, therefore, be recorded as one of the possible solutions of the problem concerning truth in religion. I have so recorded it in Chapter 4, where I try to enumerate the various alternatives that constitute possible solutions of the problem.

(xi)

Since, unlike Campbell and those who share his views, we are here concerned with truth in religion, we cannot avoid the question as to whether religions that claim logical and factual truth for their doctrines, especially for their descriptive beliefs, should be demythologized.[27]

Why should mythologies be expunged from sacred books that are the basis of religious belief in many of the world's great religions? The fact that the myths have only poetical, not logical and factual, truth does not detract from their religious significance. For something to possess meaning for us is quite independent of its having or not having factual truth. All imaginative literature has great meaning for us without having any factual truth.

If the quest for meaning and the pursuit of the truth are quite separate enterprises, then something can have meaning without being factually true. No harm is done to religions that claim factual truth for their beliefs because they also embrace the myths or mythologies with which their doctrines are associated.

There are two further points to consider here. First, the narrative passages in question may claim to be true historical accounts of the events or episodes narrated—in which case they must be judged in the light of the critical criteria for assessing the accuracy and authenticity of any narration that claims to be historical.

27. The demythologizing of the New Testament was first proposed in this century by Rudolf Bultmann. His motivation was to separate the factual truths that can be derived from correct interpretations of scriptural texts from the mythical stories that are also embedded in these texts. See Rudolf Bultmann et al., *Kerygma and Myth: A Theological Debate* (New York, 1961) in which Bultmann's proposals are severely criticized by other Protestant theologians.

Second, the fictional accounts may be recognized for what they are, as having only poetical truth. At the same time they may be understood as having religious significance *when they are properly, not just literally,* interpreted. Then there is no reason whatsoever for expunging myths that, taken as only poetically true, cannot possibly *detract from or obscure the logical and factual truth of religious doctrine.*

In the two conditions italicized above, which justify not demythologizing books that are regarded as sacred or holy, lies the only justification for an effort to rid religion of some of its myths or mythologies.

Take, for example, the New Testament story of the three wise men who came from the far corners of the earth bringing gifts to attend the nativity of Jesus in Bethlehem; and the Old Testament stories of the flood and Noah's ark and of the Tower of Babel. For those who take these stories as mythical, not historical, and who find some religious significance in them, there is no reason for expunging them. But for those who, like the fundamentalists of our time, read the words of the text literally and, hence, accept the stories as factual history rather than as fictional narratives, the removal of their self-deception can only come from showing them how to interpret the texts correctly, in a nonliteral manner.

That is of great importance *only* with respect to narrative passages, passages which, when misunderstood, result in interpretations that must be rejected because, in Augustine's terms, they come into conflict with what we know by other means. The wrong interpretation, which is usually a literal interpretation that attaches factual truth to a myth, must not be allowed to detract from or obscure the truth of the articles of faith that constitute a religion's credal commitments.

To believe, in the guise of religious faith, what is, on scientific or philosophical grounds, factually untrue is to be superstitious. Superstition is a counterfeit of religion and a perversion of it. Superstitions, like articles of faith, are beyond proof by evidence or reasons, but they are not beyond being disproved and discredited.

(xii)

Following his two principles for the interpretation of Sacred Scripture, Augustine, in my judgment, succeeded in demythologizing Genesis 1 in the fourth century A.D. The literal, fundamentalist reading of that text and the acceptance of that literal reading as containing the factual truth about God's creation of the cosmos makes an utter mockery of the Jewish, Christian, and Muslim belief in the doctrine of creation *ex nihilo* by God.

According to Augustine's understanding of God as a purely spiritual being having eternal (i.e., nontemporal and immutable) existence, Genesis 1 cannot be interpreted as a succession of creative acts performed by God in six temporal days. In Augustine's view, the creation of all things was instantaneously complete. God created all things at once *in their causes*. The *actualization* of the *potentialities* invested in those *original causes* is a natural development in the whole span of time.[28]

If Augustine were writing in the twentieth century, he would have called it an evolutionary development. The order of "six days" is not a temporal order but an order of the

---

28. See Augustine, *De Genesi ad litteram*, Bk. IV, Ch. 33, in J. P. Migne's *Patrologia Latina*, Vol. 34, p. 318, and Bk. V., Ch. 3, p. 323. See also Thomas Aquinas, *Summa Theologica*, Pt. I, Q. 74, Art. 2.

graduations of being, from lower to higher. In thus interpreting Genesis 1 in the light of twentieth-century knowledge of evolutionary development, Augustine would be following his own two rules for (1) holding on to the truth of Sacred Scripture without wavering, but also (2) holding on to an interpretation of it *only* if that accords with everything else we now know.

Demythologizing Genesis 2 and 3 is more difficult. What Augustine did with Genesis 1, someone must do with Genesis 2 and 3. If they are Christians, they must interpret the story so that it preserves basic Christian beliefs: about the moral state of the human race, a state that requires a redeemer and a savior for the salvation of the soul and the resurrection of the body. The narrative in Genesis 2 and 3 must be read so that its exegesis supports the Christian belief that God, in creating man in his own image, endowed him with free will and, thereby, with the choice between obeying or disobeying God's commandments.

The story of the Garden of Eden, of Adam and Eve and of the serpent and Lillith, may be a myth rather than true history, but this does not alter the religious significance that must be found in it when it is properly interpreted in nonnarrative terms. That is the task of the biblical exegete when he attempts to preserve the religious doctrine while removing the mythology. Demythologizing Sacred Scripture calls for profoundly daring biblical exegesis, that dares to be true to the two precepts that Augustine himself followed in demythologizing Genesis 1.

Finally, we would do well to remember Professor Campbell's reference to "metaphor as myth and as religion." We should ask ourselves why Holy Scripture is filled with metaphorical language that gives it the aspect of myth. To that question, Aquinas gives us an answer worth considering and one that Campbell should have considered.

It is befitting [for] Holy Writ to put forward divine and spiritual truths under the likenesses of material things. For God provides for everything according to the capacity of its nature. Now it is natural to man to attain to intellectual truths through sensible things, because all our knowledge originates from sense. Hence in Holy Writ spiritual truths are fittingly taught under the metaphors of [sensible] material things.[29]

In this respect, Aquinas goes on to say, Holy Writ is like poetry, but it differs from poetry in that Sacred Scripture "makes use of metaphors as both necessary and useful" for the learning of divine and spiritual truths.

---

29. Thomas Aquinas, *Summa Theologica*, Pt. I, Q. 1, Art. 9, Response and Reply to Obj. 1.

Note to Chapter 3

In his *Poetics*, Aristotle writes as follows:

It is also evident from what has been said that the task of the poet is to state, not what has [actually] occurred, but the kinds of things which might [be expected to] occur, and these are possible by virtue of their probability or their necessity. In fact, the historian differs from the poet not by stating things without rather than with meters—the writings of Herodotus would be no less a history if they were produced with meter rather than without meter—but by speaking of what has actually occurred, whereas the poet speaks of the kinds of things which are likely to occur. In view of this, poetry is both more philosophical and more serious than history; for poetry speaks rather of what is universally the case, whereas history speaks of particular events which actually occurred. (Trans. Hippocrates G. Apostle, Elizabeth A. Dobbs, and Morris A. Parslow. (Grinnell, Iowa: 1990.) Chapter 9.)

CHAPTER 4

Truth in Religion

(i)

In the preceding pages I have discussed the logic of truth only with respect to the three religions of Western origin—the three monotheistic religions that claim to have supernatural foundations and divine authority for the creeds they affirm and the rules or practices they prescribe.

We must now broaden our consideration to include the great religions of Far Eastern origin: Hinduism, Buddhism in its several distinct forms, Taoism, Confucianism, and Shintoism. Among these are religions I have classified as cosmological: religions that have explicit orthodoxies and also explicit orthopraxies, as well as religions in which only orthopraxies are explicit, but in each of which an implicit orthodoxy is presupposed.

One significant difference between the three Western religions and the six or seven major religions of the Far East concerns the line that divides religion from philosophy. In the three Western religions, the line between the domain of faith and the domain of reason is sharp and clear. There have been many controversies in the West about the relation of these two domains to one another, but there has been no doubt about their distinction from one another.

The dividing line is much less distinct in the Far East, sometimes even becoming evanescent, and almost always allowing an overlapping of the two domains. The reason for this is that, with few if any exceptions among these Far Eastern religions, their creeds and rules do not include, as a governing principle, the belief that they have a divine source in God's revelation of Himself, recorded in books regarded as holy or sacred.

With regard to the logic of truth, there is another important difference between the three Western religions and the six or seven religions of the Far East. The cultures in which the Western religions originated and developed all adopted or accepted the logic that had been formulated by the Greeks in antiquity. This is certainly true of Christianity and Islam; and while it is not true of the Judaism that predated Greek philosophy, it is true of the Jewish philosophers in the Hellenistic period and of Jewish theologians in the Middle Ages.

(ii)

Among the first principles of Greek logic is the rule governing the truth and falsity of incompatible propositions: either that both cannot be true, though both may be false, or that one must be true and the other must be false. Underlying this rule is an ontological axiom—a truth about reality—that the

Greeks thought was self-evident; namely, that nothing can both be and not be at the same time, and that nothing can both have and not have a certain specified characteristic or attribute at the same time.

Of the two presuppositions underlying the logic of truth (the first concerning the existence of an independent reality, the second concerning reality's being determinate in itself), the first is challenged by modern idealistic philosophies and the second by the Copenhagen interpretation of Heisenberg's principle of uncertainty in quantum mechanics. The realism of common sense, the realism that underlies all our daily activities, suffices, in my opinion, to dispose of the basic mistake made by idealistic philosophers.[30]

The error involved in the Copenhagen interpretation of Heisenberg's principle of uncertainty lies in one extraordinary philosophical mistake made unwittingly or defiantly by twentieth-century physicists. It is the error of restricting reality to what is measurable by physicists, attributing to reality only its measurable characteristics. As I have pointed out earlier, Stephen Hawking and others, from Einstein on, identify time with physically measurable time. Physicists may not be interested in time they cannot measure, but that is quite different from saying that unmeasurable time does not exist.

The same mistake is involved in converting Heisenberg's principle of uncertainty in our measurement of the position and velocity of a moving electron into the proposition that, at a given moment in time, the electron does not have a completely determinate velocity and position. The principle should be understood as attributing uncertainty *only* to our measurements in quantum mechanics. That uncertainty, which is epistemic, or

---

30. See Chapters 7 and 8 of my recent book, *Intellect: Mind Over Matter.*

in the field of our knowing, is fallaciously converted into an indeterminacy in the structure of reality, which then becomes ontological, not epistemic. The fact that the ontological determinateness of the electron's position and velocity is not measurable by physicists and so is of no interest to them does not mean that it has no real existence, any more than time not measurable by physicists lacks reality. The substitution of the word "indeterminacy" for the word "uncertainty" indicates the illicit conversion by the Copenhagen school of a subjective into an objective probability.[31]

(iii)

In Western logic, the laws governing the opposition of incompatible propositions are unquestioned. They are self-evident because the opposite is unthinkable. Two propositions that are contrary to each other cannot both be true though both can be false. The pursuit of truth in mathematics, science, and philosophy is governed by freedom from contradictions. Now that mathematics and science have become transcultural, one might suppose that the logic of incompatible propositions would also have become transcultural. But that is not the case. Some, if not all, of the Far Eastern cultures do not accept this rule of thought with respect to incompatibles, nor do they accept the underlying view of reality that it presupposes. It is not self-evidently true for them.

---

31. See my discussion of this point in *Six Great Ideas*, pp. 215–18. See also the note on reality in relation to quantum theory that is appended to this chapter. That note is excerpted from my book *Intellect: Mind Over Matter*, Chapter 8, pp. 105–114. As presented here, it is also improved and corrected; errors in the original have been expunged here.

On the contrary, they hold the very opposite to be true, that the guiding rule of thought should drive the mind to embrace contradiction because contradictions in their view lie at the very heart of reality. It would seem that we cannot apply the Western logic of truth to the religions prevalent in Far Eastern cultures where that logic has no authority.

In addition, in these Far Eastern cultures, there is a latent or explicit Averroism. For them, there are two distinct realms of truth: the truths of science and technology, and the truths of religious faith, of religious beliefs and rules of conduct. The fact that there may be admixtures of philosophical thought in these religious beliefs makes no difference to the point under consideration, which is that these two realms of truth do not touch or come into contact with one another because they are segregated into logic-tight compartments. In these Far Eastern cultures, such schizophrenia is regarded as a healthy state of mind. It is welcomed and espoused.[32]

It may appear to be nothing but an expression of parochial Western prejudice on my part to argue that, on these two points of logic and ontology, the Far Eastern cultures are in error. Nevertheless, I am compelled to do so. If Averroism is wrong in the West, it cannot be right in the East. If the only way to avoid the error of Averroism in the West is to regard truth in the domain of religion as merely poetical truths— truths of fiction, not of fact—then that must also be the only way to avoid the error of Averroism in the Far East.

What prevents this from being merely a parochial prejudice on my part is a fact that has become evident to everyone in

32. The espousal of Averroism in some of the cultures of the Far East may be psychologically comforting, even an escape mechanism for avoiding extremely difficult problems involving incompatible alternatives between which individuals do not want to choose.

the twentieth century but has not always been so. It is the fact that Western technology has become transcultural. It has spread from the West to the East and South. It is now globally at work.

(iv)

Wherever the fruits of technology are used, the truth of mathematics and natural science are acknowledged. If the underlying mathematics and natural science were not true, the technology would not work successfully. If the underlying mathematics and natural science are true, then the underlying view of reality as free from inherent contradictions must also be true; for if it were not, the conclusions of the empirical natural sciences could not be true by virtue of their correspondence with reality.

That there is an independent reality with which the propositions we assert can correspond or fail to correspond is assured (against the fundamental error of philosophical idealism, which in the history of Western philosophy occurred only in the last few centuries) by the way in which technologically contrived devices work or fail to work. Technology is not magic, as it would be in the world of the philosophical idealist.

The foregoing argument cannot avoid ending with a conclusion that will seem harshly illiberal to those who wish to defend unrestricted cultural pluralism. The conclusion is that the schizophrenia resulting from an Averroistic duality of truth in the domains of science and religion (where neither domain regards its truth as poetical or fictional rather than factual) is *not* a healthy state of mind and should not be welcomed and embraced.

Then, should not Western natural or philosophical theology have a direct bearing on the claims to truth on the part of some or all of the Far Eastern religions?

The conclusions of Western philosophical theology that I have in mind are: (1) God exists as the one supreme being; (2) God is transcendent and exists necessarily whether this radically contingent universe exists or not; and (3) God is the creator of this universe *ex nihilo* and the preserver of its existence at every moment that it does exist. If these conclusions are correctly judged to be factually true, then any religious faith that denies them must be factually false, at least with respect to God.

If it is possible to prove the existence of one infinite, incorporeal immutable being who is the creator of the cosmos, then that truth (even if it is not beyond the shadow of a doubt, but only beyond all reasonable doubt) amounts to a disproof of any religious belief that asserts a plurality of deities that are not the indispensable cause of the existence of the cosmos.

A similar test can be applied to the nontheistic cosmological religions of the Far East. If what these religions believe about reality and the cosmos is incompatible with the truths about the cosmos that are integral to technology and its underlying natural science, then on these points their articles of religious faith, those which make contrary factual assertions about reality and the cosmos, cannot be true.

Should philosophy ever become as transcultural as technology, mathematics, and science, the argument might be carried a step further. That branch of philosophy which is natural or philosophical theology, making no appeal to religious faith, includes, as we have seen, a proof of the existence of God, the creator of this contingent cosmos *ex nihilo*, and the preserver of its existence at every instant that it exists. If that proof were to be transculturally acknowledged, then it would call for the rejection as false of all religious beliefs to the contrary.

In other words, the great religions of the Far East would have to meet two tests for their doctrines not to be discredited. One would be their compatibility with the scientific knowledge that is now transcultural. The other would be their compatibility with the philosophical theology that had become transcultural.

But these two tests cannot become operative in the sphere of religion until the cultures of the Far East are cured of the Averroism that keeps religion and science or philosophy in logic-tight compartments.

(vii)

Let us now shift our attention to all the major religions of the world, those of Western as well as Far Eastern origin. Where does the truth lie? Is there some truth in all religions, more truth in some and less in others? Is only one of them true and all the others false? Is the one that is true completely true or may it have some errors that need to be expunged? Does the truth to be found in one religion include truths that are also found in other religions? Are all religions false, both with respect to their descriptive factual assertions and their prescriptive normative rules of conduct? Or, among religions that are false with respect to their descriptive factual assertions, may there also be some moral truths among their prescriptive rules of conduct?

All the great religions claim truth for their beliefs whether they deny that there is truth in other religions or acknowledge that there is some measure of truth in some or all of the others.

But while claiming descriptive or prescriptive truth for their beliefs, all do not assume or acknowledge the obligation to proselytize—to undertake missionary activities throughout the world aimed at converting as many individuals as possible.

Hence, to the foregoing questions, an additional question must be asked. What is the significance of the fact that, while each of the world's great religions claims truth for its factual or moral beliefs, as well as for its ceremonial and ritualistic precepts, only some religions undertake missionary activities and attempt to make converts, while others do nothing of the kind, and some even operate under the obligation not to proselytize or convert? If a religion claims truth for its beliefs, why does it not seek to universalize itself? Should not the truth its communicants espouse be shared as widely as possible?

(viii)

Questions of this sort, though not as explicitly formulated, have been the concern of two recently published books, one by Harvey Cox, a liberal Protestant student of religion, and the other by Hans Küng, a liberal Roman Catholic theologian. The Cox book is entitled *Many Mansions: A Christian's Encounter with Other Faiths*. The Küng book is entitled *Theology for the Third Millennium: An Ecumenical View*.

Little time needs to be spent on the book by Harvey Cox. It is mainly concerned with what he calls an "interfaith dialogue." The few pages in it that are devoted to the question of truth in diverse religions reveal very little understanding on Cox's part of the logic of truth. Nevertheless, he embraces the pluralism of the world's diverse religions as unalterable and even desirable. He has no hesitation in attributing some measure of truth to each and every one of them. That is how he understands the statement of Christ in the gospel according to St. John, that "in my Father's house there are many mansions."

Cox obviously interprets "my Father's house" to be the kingdom of God *in this world*, and the "many mansions" to be the *diverse religions of the world*, all true at least in some respects, no matter how incompatible they are in many other respects.

The statement by Jesus is taken from John 14. The usual interpretation of that passage is that Jesus, about to leave His disciples, is promising them that He will rejoin them after His resurrection and take them with Him to heaven, for the kingdom of heaven is open to all who believe that He is one with the Father, love Him, and keep His commandments.

The gospel texts do not support Cox's espousal of pluralism in the world's religions, nor does his mishandling of the word "truth" throw any light on his attribution of truth in some measure to all of them. When the word "truth" is used strictly in terms of the logic of truth here expounded, that attribution is plainly incorrect.

Harvey Cox tells us that he is more and more suspicious of the method of studying religion represented by Joseph Campbell and Mircea Eliade, which tends to identify the study of religion with the study of mythology.[33] But the reasons that Cox gives for his dissent have nothing to do with the fact that mythologies, being fictional narratives, make no claim to factual truth, unlike most credal religions.

Professor Cox, conceding that the question of truth in re-

---

33. See Harvey Cox, *Many Mansions: A Christian's Encounter with Other Faiths* (Boston, 1988), p. 203.

ligion cannot be avoided or evaded, refers to a contemporary student of religion, Carl Raschke, who "realized that the question of the diverse claims to truth made by the different traditions would finally have to be faced."[34] After he reviews Raschke's four methods of doing so, Professor Cox concludes with the statement: "But when one adds them all up, the question of truth is still missing."[35]

Whether Professor Cox fully understands the logic of truth is highly questionable. He is able to say that "from Jesus I have learned both that he is the Way and that in God's house there are many mansions. I do not believe these two statements are contradictory."[36] A few pages earlier, he says: "I believe [that] God can and does speak to us through people of other faiths."[37] Does this impute logical, not poetical, truth to diverse religions that contradict one another? If so, Cox would appear to be unacquainted with the logic of truth.

Hans Küng's book is no better than Cox's with respect to the logic of truth. While saying that the question of truth in religion is a "fatal question," and "there is no getting around [it],"[38] his own handling of the word "truth" permits him to say, on the one hand, that all religions are true and, on the other hand, that for a person of any one religious faith, there is only one true religion, his own.[39]

A true religion, according to Küng, "truly helps [one] to be a human being."[40] But he also speaks of a religion as

---

34. Ibid., p. 165.
35. Ibid., p. 169.
36. Ibid., p. 19.
37. Ibid., p. 17.
38. Hans Küng, *Theology for the Third Millennium* (New York, 1988), pp. 229–30.
39. Ibid., pp. 248–49.
40. Ibid., p. 243.

being false to the extent that it "manifestly oppresses, injures, and destroys human beings." In this connection, Küng cites the Hindu caste system, Islamic holy wars and cruel punishments, and the pogroms of Christian anti-Semitism. Also in this connection, Küng maintains that "the question 'What is true and what is false religion?' is identical with . . . 'What is good and what is bad religion?' "[41]

Stated in these terms, which tend to ignore or dismiss questions of factual truth and to identify truth in religion with what is morally good for its communicants to believe, as well as with conduct that is just to outsiders, Küng's attempt to think ecumenically about the plurality of religions has little bearing or no bearing on the questions with which we have been concerned.

It may have some bearing on the ecumenical union of all Christian churches, Protestant with Roman Catholics and the Roman Catholic Church with the Eastern Orthodox Church. However unlikely it is that this will occur in the near future, Küng would concede that such ecumenical union is out of the question with regard to orthodox Christianity and Orthodox Judaism, with regard to Orthodox Judaism and orthodox Islam, and with regard to orthodox Islam and Orthodox Judaism or Christianity.

The crucial defects in Hans Küng's ecumenical thinking about religion, as with Joseph Campbell's reductive thinking about religion in relation to mythology, lies in the fact that the cast of their minds has been formed and deeply influenced by their addiction to the twentieth-century liberal attitude toward pluralism and by the serious errors in modern thought, especially those made by such thinkers as Kant, Hegel,

---

41. Ibid., pp. 239, 244.

Nietzsche, Heidegger, and Freud; and in Campbell's case, of Schopenhauer and Jung.

It should also be said of both Küng and Campbell that what little understanding they have of the philosophical wisdom to be found in antiquity and the Middle Ages is everywhere tinged with modern prejudices that work in favor of what they regard as great advances made in philosophy since the eighteenth century. They are also uncritical in improperly attributing undue philosophical significance to the scientific findings of the nineteenth and twentieth centuries, particularly those made recently in the social sciences, especially cultural anthropology.

Küng also makes the mistake of thinking that the pragmatic method of testing whether a given proposition is correctly judged to be true or false eliminates the definition of truth as the agreement of the mind with reality.[42] He fails to define truth correctly and, failing that, permits himself to use the word "truth" equivocally.[43]

(ix)

If any one of the three Western religions claims descriptive factual truth for its religious beliefs or articles of faith, it must deny such truth to the orthodoxies of the other two insofar as they are incompatible. The same holds for any one of these three Western religions in relation to any of the major religions of the Far East.

---

42. Ibid., p. 229.
43. Ibid., pp. 238–39.

We see how our earlier consideration of Joseph Campbell's views about mythology and religion led us to two conclusions. Campbell, it will be remembered, made two main points: (1) mythologies do not have any factual truth, but only the kind of truth that is appropriate to poetry or fiction; and (2) a religion is a mythology incorrectly interpreted as having factual truth. It turns into a religion when it becomes the poetry in which a people believe and which they mistakenly, and superstitiously, regard as factually true.

Campbell's two conclusions were: (1) in the factual sense of truth, no religion is true; (2) in the poetical sense of truth, *all* religions are true in varying degrees. Let me state Campbell's negative conclusion in other terms: all religions are incorrect in judging to be factually true what they believe about God, the cosmos, man, the human condition, and human destiny.

It would be impossible for all of them to be correct in these judgments since their affirmations or negations about these matters are incompatible. In addition, religions may have no basis in factual truth for the rituals, ceremonies, and practices that they prescribe. However, there may still be, as we shall presently see, some prescriptive truth in the ethical precepts religions lay down for leading a morally good life and for acting righteously toward others.

But let us first return to Hans Küng. Without indicating whether he is using the word "truth" in its descriptive factual sense or in its prescriptive normative sense, Küng asks whether there is one true religion or several.[44] He then presents the following four alternatives:

---

44. Ibid., pp. 226–29.

TRUTH IN RELIGION

1. None is true.

2. Only one is true; all others are false.

3. Though only one religion is in all major respects true, other religions share in that truth.

4. Religions are all true, each true in some way.[45]

I would state the alternatives somewhat differently. One is, of course, Professor Campbell's view that none is factually true. Being mythologies, all may have some measure of poetic truth, but all are false in their factual or descriptive beliefs even though there may be some measure of prescriptive truth in their moral precepts. The other alternatives are as follows:

1. Only one of the world's great religions is completely true. All the others share some of that truth, admixing it with falsehoods or mistakes.

2. All of the world's great religions contain admixtures of truth and error, with one of them truer than any of the others. All can be graded in the degree of truth they possess from more to less.

3. With regards to its orthodoxy, the one religion that is truer than any of the others is not yet completely true, but can and should look forward to further development in which certain of its beliefs are expunged and others are added to make it, as nearly as possible, completely true.

4. With regard to its orthopraxy, a religion that is

---

45. Ibid., pp. 230–36.

false in its factual or descriptive beliefs, may be true in its moral or prescriptive beliefs.

5. While some of the world's great religions are true in certain respects and false in others, some religions are completely false.

It is at this point that Hans Küng asks us to forget the orthodoxies of the world's religions, as if they were of little importance, and to concentrate on their orthopraxies—their prescriptive and normative rules of conduct and their mandates with regard to religious rituals, ceremonies, and other practices.

Let us take note of the fact that the ceremonial and judicial precepts of the diverse religions, as well as their sumptuary or dietary dictates, are incompatible with one another. They cannot, therefore, all be true in the sense of laying down the right precepts to follow. But among the prescriptions of the great religions, there are also moral laws or rules of right behavior in the conduct of one's own life and in one's actions toward others. When we concentrate on these moral precepts, it is possible that there is much in common to all, or most, of the major religions of the world; or at least there may be less incompatibility among them with regard to these ethical precepts than in any other respect.

(x)

The precepts of the natural moral law must be the same for all human beings, everywhere and at all times, if they are inherent in human nature and discoverable by our understanding of what is really good and right for human beings to seek and to do. This is tantamount to asserting that there is only one sound, moral philosophy, one that directs each of us in leading morally good lives regardless of our individual and cultural differences. I am willing to make that assertion without hesitation.[46] There cannot be a plurality of incompatible moral doctrines all prescriptively true, any more than there can be a plurality of incompatible religious orthodoxies, all factually true.

The prescriptive truths that are common to all or most religions may have the precepts of the natural moral law at their core. They may all share in an ethics that is formulated philosophically. Some of the precepts of the natural moral law coincide with precepts of the divine law.

For example, it is a teaching of Jesus Christ that "as you would that men should do to you, do you also to them likewise." The Jewish Talmud teaches that "what is hateful to yourself, do not do to your fellow men." An Islamic teaching is that "no man is a true believer unless he desires for his brother that which he desires for himself." The Hindu *Mahabharata* declares that "one should never do to another that which one would regard as injurious to oneself." In the Buddhist sutra, we find the teaching that "as a mother cares for her son, all her days, so toward all living beings a man's mind should be all-embracing." The Confucian, Taoist, and Jainist writings contain similar precepts.

These are all slightly differing versions of the Golden Rule as a precept in moral philosophy. Two things should be pointed out about the Golden Rule. One is its vacuity as a precept of

---

46. In fact, I have done so. See the Postscript to my book *The Time of Our Lives* (New York, 1970); and also see Chapters 19 and 20 in *Reforming Education* (New York, 1989).

conduct unless it is filled in with an understanding of what is really good for any human being and, in consequence, an understanding of what is right for all others.[47]

The second point is more important. The prescriptive truth of the Golden Rule, properly understood, or the moral truth in various religious precepts that are summarized in the Golden Rule, presupposes the affirmation of some descriptive or factual truths.

The only prescriptive or moral truth that does not presuppose any descriptive or factual truths is the first principle of morality: we *ought* to seek everything that is really good for human beings and nothing else.

What then is the factual or descriptive truth that is presupposed by the Golden Rule? It is that human beings are different in kind, not just in degree, from nonhuman animals. You are not enjoined by the Golden Rule to do unto others, when they are nonhuman animals, what you would have them do unto you: first, because you know that predatory or lethally dangerous brutes are instinctively inclined to injure or kill you; and second, because treating them as you should treat other human beings would probably have disastrous consequences for you.

The prescriptive truth in moral philosophy that is common to many, if not all, of the great religions of the world is thus accompanied by a descriptive or factual truth in philosophical anthropology (i.e., that human beings differ in kind, not merely in degree, from nonhuman animals or brutes). But the fact that many of the world's greatest religions share these

---

47. In order to know how others *should* behave toward you, you must *first* know what is *really* good for you. Since everything that is really good for you is also really good for others, in terms of our common human nature and our natural needs, that controls your behavior toward them as well as theirs toward you.

philosophical truths has no bearing on their beliefs that are not philosophical—that are beyond proof but not beyond disproof.

Furthermore, to whatever extent they come into conflict in the area of prescriptive truth, the incompatible orthopraxies of diverse religions presuppose conflicting factual judgments about the structure of reality and about human nature, either explicitly declared in their orthodoxies or implicitly there.

This may lead to a satisfying conclusion for many. Most people are more concerned with practical than theoretical matters, with how to live well and act righteously than with the facts about the shape and structure of reality, visible and invisible. They will be pleased to learn that, in spite of the possibility that all religious faiths in the world may be factually false, or that only one may be factually true, nevertheless, so far as human conduct is concerned, there is a common core of sound morality and prescriptive truth in all or most of the major religions.

As for the next millennium, let us remember the prediction that Arnold Toynbee made late in his life. World government, he prophesied, would come about by conquest or by federation. It would prosper only if a world cultural community also came into existence and, with it, a universal religion adopted worldwide.

Let us also bear in mind that *if* a plurality of religions persists in the next millennium, and should Joseph Campbell be correct in thinking that, as mythologies, they can have only poetical truth, then choice among them will remain nothing but the kind of individual preference we exercise with regard to matters of taste. The kind of thinking that is requisite in dealing with matters of logical truth would be completely out of place.

(xi)

Drawing the line between philosophy and religion is much more difficult than drawing one between mythology and religion. When, in the Christian Middle Ages, philosophy was regarded as the handmaiden of theology, it served Christian dogmatic theology not only in its effort to prove the existence of God, regarded as a preamble to faith, but also in the help it provided the theologian in clarifying the dogmas of faith. At the beginning of this century, in our parochial colleges and even in our secular institutions, religion and philosophy were often grouped together as the province of one department and were often taught by the same professors. But a troublesome point arises from the distinction between some religions as supernatural knowledge and philosophy as a branch of natural knowledge, along with history and empirical science.

If all religions claimed to have supernatural sources or foundations for their creeds or articles of faith, then the line between religion and philosophy would be sharp and crystal clear. But some religions make no such claims. Their ultimate sources must, therefore, be purely human, though their founding and leading teachers may be extraordinary human beings. How, then, can one draw a line between these religions and philosophy?

The answer may be that philosophy calls for no differentiation between the sacred and the profane, the holy and the secular; philosophy has no rituals, ceremonials, sacraments; it has no forms of worship; it has no priesthood or persons who officiate at religious ceremonies and rituals; it has no hierarchy of officialdom; it has no sacred words or objects; it has no prayers. It prescribes no way of life to be followed as the means to the salvation of the spirit, here or hereafter. Moral philosophies may include rules of conduct, but they are not directed toward spiritual salvation.

Thus far we have considered religion only in its practical aspect as a body of rules and practices, as having what I earlier called an orthopraxy. But I also pointed out earlier that an orthopraxy in a religion that does not have an explicitly stated creed or articles of faith, necessarily presupposes the assertion of factual propositions upon which its rules for the conduct of life rest. Those propositions constitute its implicit orthodoxy.

How do the propositions in this orthodoxy differ from those that constitute a philosophical doctrine if they are the product of purely human resources—man's inherent natural cognitive powers? Does religious thought become identical with a philosophical enterprise?

The only answer that I can give to this difficult question turns on the presence, in a set of religious beliefs or articles of faith, of at least some that are not subject to proof by the means available for supporting the correctness of judgments about what is true in the fields of history, empirical science, and philosophy. In other words, *at least some* of the propositions affirmed in these religions are exactly like the religious beliefs in other religions that claim a supernatural source or foundation.

How that can be is something of a mystery. If the beliefs are of purely human origin, having no authority beyond what the unaided human intellect can confer upon them, then why do they behave like articles of faith that claim to have divine authority?

Furthermore, I have so far supposed that in religions that do not claim a supernatural source or foundation, only some beliefs behave, with regard to the logic and methodology of proof, in the same way as do articles of faith with divine authority. In these religions, other beliefs are expressed in statements that resemble ordinary philosophical assertions. Religion and philosophy would appear to have merged or become intertwined.

Only those religions that claim to have a supernatural source and divine authority for their articles of faith separate themselves by an unbridgeable chasm from the highest reaches of philosophical thought in that branch of metaphysics which is natural theology. Philosophical theology may carry one's mind to the edge of religious belief, but that is the near edge of a chasm that can only be crossed to the far edge by a leap of faith that transcends reason.

Note to Chapter 4

REALITY IN RELATION TO
QUANTUM THEORY

I think the matter can be further clarified by the following
considerations. In the first place, let us note Niels Bohr's
principle of complementarity, which amounts to saying that
conceiving the electron as a wave and conceiving it as a particle were not only alternative ways of conceiving it, but also
complementary ways of doing so. As Werner Heisenberg
pointed out, these are "two complementary descriptions of
the same reality. . . . These descriptions can be only partially
true; there must be limitations to the use of the particle
concept as well as of the wave concept, else one could not
avoid contradictions. If one takes into account those limitations which can be expressed by the uncertainty relations,
the contradictions disappear."[48] In other words, Bohr's
principle affirms the principle of noncontradiction as governing our thought, and it is a correct rule of thought only

---

48. Werner Heisenberg, *Physics and Philosophy: The Revolution in Modern Science*
(New York, 1958), p. 43.

if noncontradiction is an ontological principle governing reality also.[49]

In the second place, let us observe the extraordinary difference between experimental measurements performed by scientists in the realm of classical or macroscopic physics—the realm of all objects larger than the atom. Here the properties of the object being measured by the physicists are properties that inhere in the objects themselves, and would exist in reality as such whether measured by physicists or not. In other words, the physical properties of the object and the object itself are not in any way affected by their scientific measurement.[50]

The difference between quantum theory and classical physics lies in the fact that when we try to measure what is happening *inside* the atom (and thus are dealing with objects smaller than the atom), our experimental measurements are intrusive; they affect the object being studied and confer upon the subatomic entities or events the properties attributed to them. Supra-atomic physical objects or events, on the other hand, are affected by our measurements to a negligible degree. The properties assigned to subatomic objects or events are conferred upon them by the experimental measurements that quantum physicists make.

The crucial problem to be solved, which Albert Einstein tried but failed to solve, can be formulated by two alternative

49. In this same book, Heisenberg also points out that "this again emphasizes a subjective element in the description of atomic events, since the measuring device has been constructed by the observer, and we have to remember that what we observe is not nature in itself but nature exposed to our method of questioning . . . [and our] trying to get an answer from experiment by the means that are at our disposal" (ibid., p. 58).

50. For example, the measurements in the research that eventuated in the table of atomic weights did *not* confer on the atoms the weights assigned to them.

questions as follows: (1) Is the physical reality of objects and events within the interior of the atom in itself determinate in character; or (2) Is reality at the level of subatomic objects and events indeterminate in itself? If the first question is answered affirmatively then Einstein was right in maintaining that quantum theory is an incomplete account of subatomic reality.

The question was not answered satisfactorily by the thought-experiment called the "Einstein-Podolsky-Rosen Paradox." The later thinking and experimental work that led to the confirmation of the Bell theorem favors the second answer. Almost all quantum physicists today accept the answer as correct. They think that they *know* that subatomic reality is indeterminate in character. The regularities observed at the supra-atomic level, they say, arise solely from the statistical predictability of large aggregates of atoms. The indeterminacy attributed to subatomic objects and events by Heisenberg's uncertainty principles is not just their indeterminability *by us*; it is intrinsic to subatomic reality.[51]

The central questions to be answered can be formulated as follows: Are the cosmic principles of uncertainty, both in the subatomic and in the supra-atomic spheres, epistemic or ontological? Do they indicate (1) values that are *indeterminable* by us or (2) values that are in themselves *indeterminate?* Having a critical bearing on these alternatives is the fact that scientific measurements in the supra-atomic realm are not intrusive and that the uncertainty in the supra-atomic sphere is negligible

---

51. Erwin Schrödinger and Werner Heisenberg were irreconcilable on this point. Schrödinger rejected the conversion of Heisenberg's uncertainty principle into statements about real indeterminacy at the subatomic level. According to Schrödinger, the uncertainty about whether the cat in his black box was dead or alive could be resolved by opening the box and finding it to be certainly one or the other. (See Walter Moore, *Schrödinger*, New York, 1989, pp. 306–309.)

as it is not in the subatomic sphere. It might be added here that the uncertainty in the supra-atomic sphere would not have been discovered prior to the discovery of it in the subatomic sphere and that it would not have been discovered there were it not for the intrusive character of our measurements.

The two questions to which the quantum physicists think they know the right answers are philosophical, not scientific, questions—questions that, if they can be answered at all, can be answered only by thought, not by research. Unfortunately for its effect on twentieth-century thought, the quantum physicists presume to answer the questions *as if* the questions were answerable only by them in the light of their research findings. That is a serious mistake on their part. It is an egregious example of the presumption that scientists in many fields have made again and again in the twentieth century.

A brief history of the atom may help us to do the philosophical thinking that is called for. Atomic theory began in the sixth century B.C. with the physical speculations of Democritus and Leucippus. The atom was then thought to be a solid and indivisible particle of matter with no interior. That conception was espoused by such sixteenth- and seventeenth-century physicists as Galileo and Newton, and by such seventeenth- and eighteenth-century philosophers as Hobbes and Locke.

In all these centuries, from the beginning in antiquity down to the first half of the nineteenth century, the atom, thus conceived, was regarded as belonging to the realm of *entia rationis*, not to the realm of *entia reale*—that is, it was regarded a scientific fiction or theoretical construct the real existence of which had not been experimentally established. Only in the first years of the twentieth century did the experimental work on atomic radiation establish two physical facts: (1) that atoms had real physical existence; and (2) that they were not solid

96

particles of matter but had discrete interior constituents. This led a little later to the hypothesis that they might even be divisible.

During all this time, the interior of the atom was not explored by intrusive measuring devices. That occurred later in the twentieth century and led to the first atomic fission in the 1940s. Quantum mechanics—the experimental and theoretical study of the interior structure of the atom—became the great revolution in twentieth-century physics that presents us with a radical difference between subatomic and supra-atomic reality. That, philosophically, is more revolutionary than quantum mechanics itself.

Atoms really existed in all the centuries before the scientific work that established their real existence. Atoms had interiors in which physical entities existed and physical events occurred in all the centuries before these facts were scientifically established. It is certainly fair to ask what the subatomic physical reality was like in all those centuries. Was it like the subatomic reality described by twentieth-century quantum theory? Was it a physical reality having the intrinsic character of indeterminacy, or was it an intrinsically determinate physical reality like the supra-atomic reality of classical physics?

To answer that question philosophically, it is logically necessary to bear in mind one point that the quantum physicists appear to forget or overlook. At the same time that the Heisenberg uncertainty principles were established, quantum physicists acknowledged that the intrusive experimental measurements that provided the data used in the mathematical formulations of quantum theory *conferred on subatomic objects and events their indeterminate character.*

The foregoing italicized words imply that the indeterminate character of subatomic objects and events is *not* intrinsic to them, *not* properties they have quite apart from their being affected in any way by the measurements made by intrusive experimental devices.

If the cause of the indeterminate values attributed to sub-atomic objects and events in quantum theory is the intrusive and disturbing measurement of those objects and events, then *does not the elimination of that cause also eliminate its effect?*

In other words, was not the physical reality of subatomic objects determinate in all those earlier centuries when the atom existed and had an interior that the experimental measurements of quantum mechanics did not intrude upon and disturb?

The following imaginary example may help us to the philosophical answer to the question posed. Imagine a pool of water in a hermetically sealed house that has endured for centuries with no human beings ever inside it. During all that time, the character of the water in the pool is completely placid. Then suddenly human beings find the house and find a way of opening it up to outside influences such as winds; and in addition, they enter the house and jump into the pool without first looking at the surface of the water. The water in the pool affected by outside influences *and especially* by the humans jumping into the pool is disturbed and no longer has the character of complete placidity. The humans describe the pool as it appeared to them after they jumped into it and attribute to it wave motions and other properties.

Can quantum mechanics through its experimentally performed measurements be a disturbing and intrusive influence that affects the character of subatomic reality and, at the same time, can its exponents be certain that subatomic reality has the intrinsic indeterminacy that quantum theory attributes to it? Is the *unexamined* interior of the atom intrinsically indeterminate in character or is it like the determinate character of supra-atomic reality?

God knows the answer, as Einstein at the beginning of his controversy with Bohr declared when he said that God does not throw dice, which implied that the *unexamined* subatomic reality is a determinate reality.

Whether or not God knows the answer, experimental science *does not know it*. Nor does philosophy know it with certitude. But philosophy can give a good reason for thinking that subatomic reality is intrinsically determinate. The reason is that quantum theorists repeatedly acknowledge that their intrusive and disturbing measurements are the cause of the indeterminacy they attribute to subatomic objects and events. It follows, therefore, that that indeterminacy cannot be intrinsic to subatomic reality.

Unfortunately, in this century, quantum theory has inadvertently given undue comfort to the worst tendency in contemporary thought—its philosophical idealism or constructivism, which denies a reality that exists in complete independence of the human mind and that has whatever intrinsic character it has without being affected by how the human mind knows it or thinks about it.[52]

To sum up: quantum theory is a theory of the examined interior of the atom. The scientific examination of that interior is, according to quantum theory, an intrusive disturbance of what is going on there. It follows that further developments of quantum theory and additional scientific investigation cannot tell us about the character of the unexamined atomic interior.

Einstein was right that quantum theory is an incomplete

---

52. The great English mathematician G. H. Hardy has a comment on this worth quoting. He writes: "It may be that modern physics fits best into some framework of idealistic philosophy—I do not believe it, but there are eminent physicists who say so. Pure mathematics, on the other hand, seems to me a rock on which all idealism founders: 317 is a prime, not because we think so, or because our minds are shaped in one way rather than another, but *because it is so*, because mathematical reality is built that way." G. H. Hardy, *A Mathematician's Apology* (Cambridge, 1940), p. 130.

account of subatomic reality. But he was wrong in thinking that that incompleteness could be remedied by means at the disposal of science. Why? Because the question that quantum theory and subatomic research cannot answer is a question for philosophy, not for science.

CHAPTER 5

Recapitulation and Conclusion

(i)

In summarizing the main points of my argument, I will not
follow the precise order in which they were made in the preceding chapters. I will omit any reference to the polemical
passages in which I criticized the views concerning mythology
and religion advanced in recent books by Wendy Doniger
O'Flaherty, Joseph Campbell, Harvey Cox, and Hans Küng
and will limit my summary to the statement of the few essential
points that readers should bear in mind. They are as follows:

1. Pluralism is desirable and tolerable in perpetuity
    a. In all matters of taste, personal preference, and
       predilection, and in expressions of individual likes
       and dislikes;
    b. In all matters of public policy and legislation,
       concerning which reasonable men can disagree and

about which decisions that must be made require
appealing to a majority vote;

c. And with regard to myths, fictional narratives, and
even religions that claim to have only poetical, not
logical or factual, truth.

2. Pluralism may be tolerated under conditions in which
matters of logical and factual truth are disputed and in
which the dispute remains unresolved, but not in
perpetuity; for with regard to such matters the
ultimate goal to be sought is agreement, not diversity
of opinion.

3. Utterances are in the realm of poetical truth if they are
about what is possible and if they are not subject to
contradiction. In contrast, utterances that are about
what is actually the case and are subject to
contradiction are in the realm of logical and factual
truth.

a. In the realm of discourse where poetical truth is to
be found, utterances can have maximum diversity
without any incompatibility.

b. In the realm of discourse where logical and factual
truth is to be found, utterances that are contrary or
contradictory are incompatible. The truth of one
excludes the truth of the other, whereas one
utterance that is poetically true never excludes
another from also being poetically true, no matter
how divergent the two utterances may be.

4. With regard to truth in religion and truth in science
or philosophy, there are three positions:

a. That of the Arabic philosopher Averroës in his
dispute with Algazeli: The truths of religious belief

and the truths of science or philosophy are not truths of the same kind. The former are truths of the imagination and are poetically true; the latter are truths of reason and are logically and factually true. Therefore, they cannot come into conflict or be incompatible.

b. That of the Christian theologian Aquinas in his dispute with the Latin Averroists of his day: The truths of faith and the truths of reason are truths of the same kind; they are logical and factual truths. Any apparent conflict between what religious belief claims to be true and what science or philosophy claims to be true must be capable of resolution because no incompatibility can exist in the realm of logical and factual truth.

c. The third position is that of "Averroism," when this term is used in a disapprobative sense for those who, finding it impossible to reconcile the truths of religion with the truths of science, keep them separate in logic-tight compartments in order not to confront their incompatibility.

5. Religious beliefs or articles of religious faith cannot be proved or established as true by the marshaling of reasons or by the amassing of evidence, but they can be disproved or discredited by being shown to be incompatible with the established truths of science or philosophy.

6. To believe that which is not only beyond proof but is also discredited by established knowledge to the contrary is superstitious, not religious, belief.

7. At this juncture in the world's history, mathematics,

the exact sciences, and technology are transcultural: what logical and factual truth they have is the same globally. History, the social sciences, and philosophy are not yet transcultural, but may become so. Until they do, the established knowledge to be found in the natural sciences serves to test the claims of religious beliefs to be logically and factually true, as well as similar claims made by this or that philosophical doctrine.

8. Among the major religions of the world (named on page 48 of Chapter 3), all of which conform to the proposed definition of religion (given on pages 45–46 of Chapter 3), only three religions claim to have a supernatural foundation to be found in a sacred scripture that purports to be a divine revelation.

   a. The three religions distinguished by this claim are Judaism, Christianity, and the religion of Islam.

   b. Among the other religions that satisfy the requirements set forth in the definition of religion, only some claim to have logical and factual truth, but the truth they claim to have is of human, not divine, origin.

(ii)

The central question in this book is where does the truth lie among the plurality of the world's organized and institution-alized religions.

The foregoing chapters have not answered that question decisively. An array of possible answers has been set forth, among which only one can be the right answer. However, the principles requisite for finding the right answer have been presented. These principles apply only to those religions that claim logical and factual truth for their doctrinal beliefs and other moral precepts. These religions are not content to have their beliefs regarded as possessing only poetical truth—the mode of truth appropriate to fictional narratives and mythologies.

Any religion that claims factual truth for itself necessarily subjects itself to the logical principles that govern all affirmations and denials in the sphere of such truth. This applies with exactly the same force to religions of Far Eastern origin as it does to religions of Western origin. This is tantamount to maintaining that the Averroism condemned by Aquinas is a mistake to be avoided in the Far East as well as in the West.

If the Averroism that is explicit in Far Eastern cultures is abandoned, religious beliefs incompatible with scientific knowledge cannot be kept in logic-tight compartments in order to avoid the logical obligation to resolve that conflict in favor of scientific truth and thus discard religious beliefs that are incompatible with it.

With these points in mind, here are two principles and three other considerations that should be employed in order to reach a decisive determination of where the truth lies among the world's religions.

(iii)

1. *The principle of the unity of truth*: All the diverse parts of the whole of truth must be compatible with one another regardless of the diversity of the ways in which these parts of truth are attained or received.

2. *The principle of transculturality*: At a given time, the truths of technology, mathematics, and the exact natural sciences are transcultural; whatever else claims to be true should also become transcultural if it is found to be compatible with the scientific truths that are now transcultural.

3. To become transcultural, a body of religious beliefs and precepts must be compatible, at a given time, with the established scientific truths that are now transcultural.

4. To become transcultural, philosophical doctrines must also be compatible, at a given time, with the established scientific truths that are now transcultural.

5. When philosophy becomes as transcultural as the established science with which it is compatible, the truths established by philosophical theology should serve as the most decisive criterion whereby to discover where the truth lies among the religions of the world.

(iv)

If the chapters of this book were a series of lectures and if the lectures were to close with the foregoing remarks, to be followed by a question period, I would expect to be asked which of the world's religions I thought could rightfully claim to be true or, if not completely true, truer than any other.

My answer would be, first of all, that I interpreted the question as asking for my judgment as a philosopher, and not for an expression of personal religious belief. The lectures, I would say, had been delivered as an effort to think philosophically about truth in religion and not as an exercise in apologetics for one religion or another. The question period should therefore be conducted in the same manner.

In answering the question as a philosopher, I would have the foregoing principles in mind: especially the principle of the unity of truth and the principle of transculturality. To these I would add three other considerations: (1) that in my view of philosophy it should become as transcultural as the scientific knowledge with which it is compatible; (2) that the branch of philosophy that is philosophical theology would then also become transcultural; and (3) that this branch of philosophy should be crucially decisive with regard to truth in religion, especially the truth of the beliefs or creeds that claim logical and factual truth.

In the light of these principles and considerations, I would be compelled to say that there cannot be logical and factual truth in any of the Far Eastern religions that are cosmological rather than theological in their orthodoxies, nor in any of the theological religions that are polytheistic rather than monotheistic.

This answer, I would add, is based on the conclusions reached in my book *How to Think About God*, in which I concluded that the existence of a single supreme being could be proved, beyond a reasonable doubt; and that the proof involved the understanding of that supreme being as the indispensable creative or exnihilating cause of a cosmos that was capable of not existing because it was capable of being otherwise than it is.[53]

The proof of God's existence in philosophical theology does not establish the religious belief in God, a belief that involves the love of God, prayer for God's grace, and other religious

---

53. Adler, *How to Think About God*, Part Five.

commitments. These require a leap of faith that goes beyond a rational argument for God's existence to belief in the God of the three Western monotheistic religions.[54]

So far, I have answered the question only in terms of those articles of faith that are credal assertions. I have not commented on the orthopraxies of the world's religions as distinguished from their orthodoxies. The prescriptions or precepts that are ceremonial and ritualistic differ from one religion to another and are, for the most part, in conflict with one another. That is not the case with respect to their moral prescriptions. Here there is much that is common to all or most of the world's religions; for the precepts of the natural, moral law must be the same for all human beings, everywhere and at all times.[55]

We are thus confronted with the further question that inevitably follows from the answer so far given: where does the truth lie in the three monotheistic religions of Western origin—in Judaism, in Christianity, or in the religion of Islam?

If any one of these religions is true in all its credal assertions, the other two cannot be true in some of theirs; for Judaism denies what Christianity and Islam assert, Christianity denies what Judaism and Islam assert, and Islam denies what Christianity and Judaism assert. Each claims the whole truth for itself and rejects similar claims by the other two. While claiming the whole truth for itself, each concedes part of the truth to the other two. There are a few credal assertions common to all three. Although the three religions differ in their ceremonial and ritualistic precepts, they share common ground in some of their moral precepts.

Hence one cannot say that one of these three religions is

54. Ibid., Chapters 17–18.
55. See Chapter 4, Section (iv), p. 74

true and the other two are false. We can only say that one of these religions is truer than the other two, and that the two that are less true share in the truth to be found in the one that is truer.

Other criteria for deciding which of the three is truer than the other two might be considered. One involves the matter of proselytizing: Should not a religion that claims logical and factual truth for its orthodoxy engage in missionary efforts to convert others to its beliefs?

Another criterion is the differing eschatology of these three religions—their views about the ultimate destiny of the individual human being or of mankind as a whole, their views about immortality, and about life after death, about divine rewards and punishments, and about salvation.

Still another is the difference in their views concerning the immanence as well as the transcendence of the supreme being.

A fourth criterion of the greatest importance is the extent to which God's self-revelation involves mysteries—mysteries, not miracles. Mysteries are articles of religious faith that exceed our natural human powers of knowing and understanding. They may be intelligible in themselves, but they are not completely intelligible to us.

It is extremely difficult to deal with these four criteria in purely philosophical terms. Therefore, I will not employ them in answering the question.

One final historical comment is relevant. We know that great theologians, both medieval and modern, in the tradition of each of these three religions have been convinced of the possibility of defending the compatibility of their faith with the scientific knowledge available at the time. In light of that fact, it is prudent for a philosopher to suspend judgment with regard to which of these religions is the truer and which the less true.

As a philosopher concerned with truth in religion, I would

like to hear leading twentieth-century theologians speaking as apologists for Judaism, Christianity, and Islam engage in a disputation. The question at issue would be which of these three religions had a greater claim to truth. It being conceded that each has a claim to some measure of truth, which of the three can rightly claim more truth than the other two?

APPENDICES

APPENDICES

The Unity of Man and the Unity of Truth

(Excerpts from a Lecture Delivered at the
Aspen Institute in 1973)

(1)

Let me begin by stating the problem as I see it. It is generated by three theses, which I hope you will agree are indisputable. The first is that the human race is a single biological species, renewed generation after generation by the reproductive determinations of a single gene pool. Hence, man is one in nature—that is, in specific nature. All individual members of the species have the same species-specific properties or characteristics.

The second thesis is that the human race being one, the human mind is also one. I am here using the word "mind" to signify the complex of cognitive and ratiocinative powers and propensities that, when exercised, result in human thought and knowledge, in social institutions, and in the productions of the arts and of technology. The human mind, thus understood, is a species-specific property: it is to be found in every individual member of the species, and it is the same in all.

The fact that mind, in the sense indicated, is subject to variations in degree (some individuals having its constituent powers to a higher, some to a lower degree), does not negate the proposition that the same powers, to whatever degree, are possessed by all human beings.

However, the truth of this thesis does preclude the notion that there is, within the human species, a primitive mind that is characteristically different from a civilized one, or an Oriental mind that differs in kind from an Occidental one, or even a child mind that differs in kind, not just degree, from an adult one. What I have just said is, I take it, a fundamental thesis of a movement called "Structuralism," which has a current vogue but which, if I understand it correctly, is based on an insight that can hardly be regarded as novel, however novel may be the particular psychological discoveries of Jean Piaget and the particular anthropological discoveries of Claude Lévi-Strauss, from which the movement draws its inspiration.

My third thesis is that world peace is an ultimate desideratum—not as an end in itself but rather as an indispensable means or condition prerequisite to the achievement of a good human life by all human beings in some future generation. The propositions that I must now add to that thesis, I hope you will agree with as much as you agree with the thesis itself: (1) that world peace is impossible without world government; (2) that world government is impossible to establish and, even if established, would not long endure and prosper without world community; and (3) that world community requires a certain degree of cultural unity or unity of civilization, a condition that certainly does not exist at present.

In the light of these initial theses, and the propositions attendant upon the third, I can now state the problem that I would like to present to you. It concerns the kind and degrees of cultural unity required for world community as a basis for world government and world peace. It involves two questions. One asks how much cultural diversity should and will persist after enough cultural unity is achieved to create a world community. Stated another way, this question is: How much cultural diversity is compatible with the unity of man and the unity of truth? The second question then follows: What kind of cultural unity is demanded by the unity of truth; and, therefore, what kind of cultural diversity is precluded?

Both questions, you will have noted, make reference to the unity of truth, a term I have suddenly introduced into the discussion and connected with the term that summarizes my first thesis—the unity of man. While you may agree with my first thesis about the unity of man, and even with its immediate consequence—the unity of the human mind—you may justly wonder whether I have not slipped a ringer into the discussion by adding the unity of truth as a third term to that pair. I will presently explain that third term and try to show you that it is inseparable from the other two members of the triad.

Before I do so, let me call your attention to another point that I mentioned just a moment ago that may also need a little substantiation. I said that the cultural unity or unity of civilization that is indispensable to world community does not exist at present and has never existed in the past. To support that statement, I need only remind you of the cultural diversities that have been and still are divisive of mankind, represented by the following dichotomies: Greek vs. barbarian; the Middle Kingdom vs. barbarian; Jew vs. Gentile; Christian vs. infidel; civilized vs. primitive man; and East vs. West or West vs. East. In all such divisions, one side claims to be the possessor of truth and light, and the other is regarded as being in error and in outer darkness. So long as such divisions persist, a world civilization or culture and a world community will not come into existence.

115

Can they be overcome? And, if so, how shall they be overcome? That is the problem we face. As I see it, the key to the solution of this problem lies *in principle* in the unity of truth —the term that I added to the unity of man and the unity of the human mind and said constituted an indissolvable triad. Now let me see if I can explain what I mean by the unity of truth. To begin with, I had better say a word about truth itself.

In the history of Western thought (please note that I am compelled to say "Western" here), a profound understanding of truth has prevailed from the time of Plato and Aristotle to the present. This understanding rests upon a single supposition; namely, that there exists, quite independent of the human mind, a reality which the human mind thinks about and tries to know. On that supposition, the truth consists in our thinking that that which is, is; and that which is not, is not. Our thinking is in error or false when we think that which is, is not; or that which is not, is. In the field of veracity and prevarication, we tell the truth when we say that we believe or think, and we tell a lie when we say the opposite of what we think or believe. This led Josiah Royce to quip that a liar is a person who willfully misplaces his ontological predicates, putting "is" where he should put "is not," or the reverse. In contrast to the liar, a person honestly in error is one who unintentionally misplaces his ontological predicates, and the correction of error consists in getting them straight—saying "is" where "is" is required, and "is not" where "is not" is required.

Thus defined, the human mind has a grasp on the truth to whatever extent the judgments it makes agree with or conform to reality—to the way things are or are not. To say this does not involve us in claiming that the human mind has a firm, final, and incorrigible grasp on any truth, though I personally think that there is a relatively small number of self-evident truths on which our grasp is firm, final, and incorrigible. However that may be, we must acknowledge that truth is *in principle* attainable, even though we may never in fact actually attain it. Otherwise, it would be unreasonable for us to engage in the pursuit of truth. That pursuit would be futile and self-defeating if, in the course of it, we did not manage to achieve approximations to the truth—statements that, while not indubitably true, are nearer to the truth, better than, truer than the statements that they correct and replace.

To this conception of the truth, whether fully possessed or only approximated, I must add one other insight that again I am compelled to say is typically Western. It is related to the supposition that I said a moment ago underlies the conception of truth as consisting in the mind's agreement with reality, the supposition; namely, that there is a reality independent of the mind with which the mind's judgments can agree or disagree. The additional insight expands that supposition to include the point that this independent reality is determinate. Either a particular thing exists or it does not exist; either it has a certain characteristic or it does not have a certain characteristic. It cannot both be and not be at one and the same time; it cannot have and not have a certain characteristic at one and the same time.

If such determinateness did not obtain in reality, it would follow that the statement that something *is* the case and the statement that it *is not* the case could both be true at the same time. If, according to our conception of truth, both of two contradictory statements (one asserting "is" and the other "is not") cannot be true at the same time, the determinateness of reality must be presupposed. In short, the principle of noncontradiction holds for both thought and reality, and it holds for thought because it holds for reality. (To this I must add the parenthetical observation that, in the controversy between Einstein and Bohr over quantum theory, Einstein was, in my

117

judgment, philosophically sounder than Bohr. The Heisenberg principle of indeterminacy has epistemological, not ontological, significance. It should be interpreted as indicating the indeterminacy of our measurements in subatomic physics, not the indeterminacy of reality in that area. Reality may be indeterminable with certainty, but this does not mean it is certainly indeterminate. The fact that we cannot assign an equally definite position and velocity to an electron in motion does not mean that the electron really lacks a completely definite position and velocity.)

With this conception of truth and with the principle of noncontradiction as an essential part of it, I can now explain what I mean by the unity of truth. It is merely an extension, but nonetheless a very important extension, of the principle of noncontradiction. To affirm the unity of truth is to deny that there can be two separate and irreconcilable truths which, while contradicting of one another and thought to be irreconcilably so, avoid the principle of noncontradiction by claiming to belong to logic-tight compartments. Thus, for example, one approach to the conflicts between religion and philosophy, or between science and either philosophy or religion, is to claim that these are such separate spheres of thought or inquiry, employing such different methods or having such different means of access to the truth, that the principle of noncontradiction does not apply. One thing can be true in religious belief and quite another, though contradictory of it, can be true in scientific or philosophical thought. . . .

(2)

The criteria of truth and falsity do not apply to all areas of human culture, but wherever they do apply, there we should expect the unity of truth to prevail and be troubled if it does not. By the same token, in the area of matters to which the criteria of truth and falsity do not apply, cultural diversity is fitting and proper. Two examples, drawn from opposite extremes of the scale, will illustrate this basic distinction.

On the one hand, mathematics is an area in which the criteria of truth and falsity are universally thought to apply; it is also an area in which the transcultural character of truth is universally acknowledged. On the other hand, cuisine is a matter of taste not of truth, and so in matters of cuisine we expect and are not at all troubled by cultural diversity. It is appropriate to speak of French, Italian, and Chinese cuisines and to express a preference for one or another that we do not expect others to share; but it is not appropriate to speak of French, Italian, or Chinese mathematics (except in a purely historical sense). Any mathematical theorem or demonstration that is true commands an assent that transcends all national and cultural divisions.

I have just said that in whatever sphere of human judgment it is proper to apply the criteria of truth and falsity, we can and should expect agreement about what is true or false to transcend all the national and cultural divisions of mankind. I must add at once that such agreements may exist in different degrees. There is a stronger and a weaker bond of agreement. The stronger, which I will call "doctrinal agreement," exists when, at a given time, those who are competent to judge agree about what is to be regarded as true, or at least a better approximation to the truth, and expect the propositions thus regarded to receive universal assent until better—truer—propositions are advanced. The weaker, which I will call "dialectical agreement," exists when those who are competent to judge disagree about what is to be regarded as true, but who, nevertheless, being persuaded that the truth is in principle attainable, are at least united in their acceptance of certain logical procedures for resolving their doctrinal disagreements and thus carrying on cooperatively the pursuit of truth.

There are two cultural areas in which we have universally acknowledged the existence of a large measure of doctrinal agreement. They are mathematics and the experimental sciences, together with their applications in technology. There are two other cultural areas in which doctrinal agreement does not exist, not even within the single cultural tradition of the West; *a fortiori*, certainly not in the world, embracing four or five distinct cultural traditions in the Far East as well as that of Western civilization.

I have in mind here the areas of religion and of philosophy, including moral and political philosophy as well as the philosophy of nature and metaphysics. The question, to which I will return presently, is whether in these two areas it is appropriate to apply the criteria of truth and falsity and, therefore, to expect agreement in at least its weaker form. If not, then religion and philosophy fall across the line that divides the cultural areas to which the criteria of truth and falsity apply and those to which they do not. Religion and philosophy then become like those matters in which the criterion of taste rather than truth is applicable—such matters as conventions or customs, languages, dress and cooking, social manners, and the fine arts. Since there is no disputing about matters of taste, we cannot even expect dialectical agreement in the sphere of our judgments about the fine arts any more than we can expect it in the sphere of our preferences with regard to cuisines.

The question, I repeat, is, On which side of the line of demarcation do religion, metaphysics, and ethics fall? Do they belong with mathematics and experimental science on that side of the line where the criteria of truth and falsity are applicable? Or do they belong with aesthetic judgments and preferences as to cuisine, dress, and manners on that side of the line where there is no disputing matters of taste, and cultural diversity should be expected to prevail?

There may be matters which *appear* to straddle the line of demarcation between the unity and the universality of truth and the plurality and singularity of tastes. Prudential judgments in the sphere of morals may be matters of this sort, partaking both of the objective and the subjective. So, too, in the sphere of social institutions, customs and positive laws may have both a natural basis and a conventional or voluntary determination, and so may partake of the universality of the natural and necessary as well as the singularity of the conventional and contingent.

However, whatever is infected, even in the slightest degree, with singularity or subjectivity falls on the side of taste rather than on the side of truth. In terms of the controlling question with which we are here concerned (namely, what elements of unity should we expect or demand in a culture and what latitude should be allowed for cultural pluralism?), those cultural elements that are *partly* matters of taste as well as those elements that are *wholly* matters of taste are matters about which we should tolerate cultural pluralism. Pluralism is intolerable only with respect to matters that are *wholly* or *purely* matters of truth—for example, mathematics.

If the criteria of truth and falsity are not applicable to philosophy and religion, we have no troublesome problem to solve; for these disciplines are then no different from such matters as cuisine, dress, and the fine arts. We can and should expect pluralism or diversity rather than unity to prevail with respect to them, not only as between the Far East and the West, but also within the Western tradition itself. If religion or philosophy is nothing but "a way of life," as it is sometimes said, or if it has no cognitive character or basis, then why should there not be as great a diversity of religions or philosophies on earth as there are cuisines, habits of dress, or languages? We do have a problem, however, and an extremely difficult one, if philosophy and religion, claiming to be true in the same sense as mathematics and experimental science, claim that truth is in varying measures approximated and, at least in principle, fully attainable in their spheres of thought and inquiry.

Let us make the assumption that presents us with a problem. Let us assume that philosophy and religion do claim cognitive status for themselves—that is, aspire to be knowledge and, therefore, subject themselves to the criteria of truth and falsity. What consequences follow from this assumption?

On that assumption, mathematics and science are necessarily only part of the whole truth—the truth that we seek to learn about the world, about nature, society, and man. On that assumption, philosophy and religion constitute additional portions or segments of the whole of the truth to be attained. Now, staying within the boundaries of Western civilization or culture, the principle of the unity of truth entails the consequence that the several parts of the one whole of the truth to be attained must coherently fit together. As we have already seen, there cannot be irreconcilable contradictions between one segment of the whole of truth and another. What is regarded as true in philosophy and religion must not conflict with what is regarded as true in science.

Moreover, since it is only in the spheres of mathematics and experimental science that doctrinal agreement has been achieved in large measure, if not completely, the truths agreed upon in those areas *at a given time* test the claims to truth that are made in philosophy and religion—areas in which doctrinal agreement has not been achieved to any appreciable degree. In other words, a particular religious belief or philosophical view must be rejected as false if, at a given time, it comes into conflict with the scientific truths agreed upon at that time. It is worth noting that two of the greatest philosophers and theologians in the Western tradition—Augustine and Aquinas—fully accepted this mandate, and they did so because they fully accepted the principle of the unity of truth and regarded the criteria of truth and falsity as applicable to philosophy and religion.

To say that there is one whole of truth all the parts of which must coherently and consistently fit together does not preclude the parts from being different from one another in a variety of ways—with respect to the objects with which they are concerned, with respect to the methods by which inquiry is conducted, and with respect to the sources or bases of the truth being sought. The truth being sought may be about numbers or justice, about natural phenomena or God; the truth being pursued may be sought by investigative procedures or by armchair reflection, by ratiocinative processes, by intuition, or even by mystical contemplation; its sources may lie in experience or in divine revelation. No matter how diverse may be the objects, methods, and sources involved in the different parts of truth, they all remain, nevertheless, parts of one whole, and as such coherently and consistently fit together.

So far, as I indicated above, I have stayed within the boundaries of Western civilization. Now let us broaden the scope of our discussion to include the whole of mankind—all human cultures, East and West. Wherever the fruits of technology are used or enjoyed, the truth of science and mathematics is tacitly acknowledged. The fruits of technology are now used or enjoyed all over the world—in the Far East as well as the West. It follows, therefore, that the truth of science and mathematics is acknowledged all over the world. It is the only part of the whole of truth that is common to the Far East and the West. The same mandate that has been operative within the

Western tradition should, therefore, be operative when we go beyond the Western tradition and consider the philosophies and religions of the Far East as well as the philosophies and religions of the West.

Just as, within the Western tradition, the truth of mathematics and science that are agreed upon at a given time have been employed as the test for accepting or rejecting Western religious beliefs or philosophical views, so, in exactly the same way, they should be employed as the test for accepting or rejecting Far Eastern religious beliefs or philosophical views. The principle holds that whatever is inconsistent or incompatible with the truths of mathematics and science that are agreed upon *at a given time* must, *at that time* be rejected as false. The principle is universally applicable—to Far Eastern as well as to Western culture. Its universal applicability is assured by the universal assent to the truths of mathematics and science from which the products of technology are derived.

The only way in which this consequence can be avoided is to remove Far Eastern religions and philosophies from the picture by regarding them as making no cognitive claims at all—that is, by putting them along with cuisines, manners, and the fine arts on the other side of the line of demarcation that divides those areas of human culture to which the criteria of truth and falsity are applicable from those areas which are concerned with matters of taste rather than truth. . . .

(3)

In conclusion, I would like to add a number of supplementary observations that point up the general tendency of the foregoing analysis and argument.

In the first place, you should now be able to see why I think it is unwise to combine selections from Far Eastern and Western literature in a single reading list or set of books, especially if they consist of materials that are essentially philosophical or religious. The issues dealt with in seminar discussions of such books are about matters to which the criteria of truth and falsity are applicable. The seminar discussions should be conducted with this in mind.

Even though basic disagreements among the authors read and among the participants are not resolved in the course of the seminar, the discussions should occur within the framework of enough dialectical agreement to render them fruitful rather than futile. The authors as well as the participants should all be talking to one another in a dialogue that represents a single universe of discourse. But, as I have pointed out, no dialectical agreement exists at present between the West and the various cultures of the Far East. Far Eastern and Western authors may appear to be talking to one another, but we are deceiving ourselves if we think that that is the case. If Far Eastern and Western authors are not engaged in dialogue with one another, then we cannot generate a fruitful discussion by reading them together.

My second concluding remark deals with an objection that might be raised to the basic presuppositions of my argument. That objection would probably run as follows: my argument presupposes the correctness of the Western view of reality and of truth as governed by the principle of noncontradiction. That is the basis of everything that has been said about the unity of truth. Some, if not all, Far Eastern thought holds a different view—that reality is at its very core made up of contradictions and that we can approximate the truth only to the extent that we are able to embrace affirmations and denials or contradictory statements about reality.

My answer to this objection is twofold. On the one hand, I must remind you that the Far East as well as the West accepts the truths mankind has so far achieved in mathematics and science, even as they use the products of technology that are based on these truths. The logic underlying the achievement of truth in mathematics and science presupposes the truth of the principle of noncontradiction, as applied to reality itself and to the judgments men make about it. Far Eastern thought can escape from the consequences of this only by being intellectually schizophrenic. On the other hand, if the Far East insists that the truths of mathematics and science are superficial, however useful they may be, and that philosophy or religion which aims to get at the heart of reality must violate the principle of noncontradiction because reality at heart is contradictory through and through, then there can be no dialogue between the Far East and West on the philosophical or religious plane, for there is not sufficient dialectical agreement to carry on an intelligible and fruitful conversation.

The third observation that I would like to make in conclusion has to do with the distinction between objectivity and subjectivity. Everything that I have said about the unity of truth, and about the distinction between doctrinal and dialectical agreement, applies only to matters that are subject to the criteria of truth and falsity and the principle of noncontradiction. This, in my view, is the realm of the objective in human life. In sharp contrast to it is the realm of the subjective—the realm of feeling and personal predilection, with respect to which, like matters of taste, there is no disputing and no adjudication by logical means.

A book by Theodore Roszak, *Where the Wasteland Ends*, criticizes Western civilization for its almost pathological addiction to objectivity and its underevaluation of the subjective aspects of human life. Roszak makes the mistake of arguing not merely for the recognition and enlargement of the subjective, but also for giving it dominance over the objective. That is hardly the right prescription if, as I think is the case, the objective and the subjective are not rival claimants for the dominant role in human life and culture, but are rather supplementary to each other, each enriching human life and culture in its own characteristic way.

This leads me to suggest that one possible view of the most profound difference between the Far East and the West is that the West has made what is by far the major contribution to the advancement of mankind in the realm of the objective, whereas the East has made a comparably great but quite different contribution to the advancement of mankind in the realm of the subjective. Thus viewed, there is no conflict between them, for there cannot be any conflict between areas of culture in which the criteria of truth and falsity are applicable and areas of culture in which these criteria are not appropriate at all.

In the fourth place, I submit the concluding observation that cultural diversity should be tolerated (i.e., accepted as unavoidable) only in those areas in which the criteria of truth and falsity and the principle of noncontradiction do not apply—that is, in the areas concerned with matters of taste (with conventions or customs in eating and in dress, with social manners, with styles in the fine arts) and also in every aspect of human life that is subjective rather than objective.

What I call "culturism"—the acceptance or, worse, the promotion and defense of cultural diversity without observing the line of demarcation between matters of truth and matters of taste, or between the realms of the objective and the subjective—is, in my judgment, as deplorable as nationalism, for both are irremediably divisive of mankind and present obstacles to a world cultural community and, therefore, to world government and world peace. Cultural differences, in those areas in which they are acceptable, or rightly to be tolerated, are all superficial. They represent a diversity in the nurture of human beings that overlays the essential or specific unity of human nature—the biological unity of man and the psychological unity of the human mind.

A great new epoch in the history of mankind lies ahead of us in the next millennium. It will not begin until there is a universal acknowledgment of the unity of truth in all the areas of culture to which the standard of truth is applicable; for only then will all men be able to live together peacefully in a world cultural community under one government. Only then will world civilization and world history begin. Such unification of mankind, called for by the biological unity of the species, will not preclude the persistence until the end of time of cultural diversity in all matters where such diversity is appropriate, as well as the persistence of philosophical or religious pluralism as long as men are engaged in the pursuit of the whole truth that, while attainable in principle, is not likely ever to be fully attained.

Cultural Unity and
Cultural Pluralism

(Excerpts from a Lecture Delivered at
International House in Tokyo in 1978)

Let me begin by stating the problem with which we are here
concerned and by indicating what I think is the key to its
solution.

The human race is a single biological species, all of its
individual members the procreated products of one gene pool,
in consequence of which all members of the species have the
same species-specific properties, possessing them in common
though possessing them in individually differing degrees.

This unity of man—this common set of species-specific
properties—underlies all genetically determined individual
differences, which are differences in the degree to which all
individual members of the species possess the same properties
which make them all human and equal as human.

This unity of man also underlies all differences that are
caused by differences in nurture and by differences in culture.

If the human race is one, all its members participating in
the same common humanity, the human mind, is also one.
As one of the species-specific properties, human mentality is

the same in all members of the species. Man being one, should not the ultimate desideratum of human life on earth be the formation of a single cultural community to which all men belong?

My answer to this question is affirmative for two reasons. First, because world peace is impossible without world government; and second, because world government is impossible without world community. If that answer is correct, we are led to the further proposition that the existence of world community requires a certain degree of cultural unity—unity of civilization.

These things being so, the problem to be solved can be stated as follows: What are the kinds and the degrees of cultural unity that are required for world community as a basis for world government? How much cultural diversity or pluralism should persist? How much is appropriate and tolerable? What is the basis for determining the matters with regard to which it is reasonable to expect worldwide cultural unity, as well as the basis for determining the matters with regard to which cultural diversity or pluralism should be tolerated because it is not incompatible with the unity of mankind and of the human mind?

The key to the solution of the problem as stated is to be found, in my judgment, in a fundamental difference between matters that belong to the sphere of truth and matters that belong to the sphere of taste, together with the moral obligations imposed upon us by our commitment to the pursuit of truth with regard to all matters that properly fall in the sphere of truth.

We must also take account of a principle that should regulate our pursuit of truth: the principle that the sphere of truth is itself unified, that it is not divisible into a plurality of separate and incompatible domains.

In addition, we must also consider the distinction between a strong and a weak form of intellectual unity or community with regard to matters that properly belong in the sphere of truth. The strong form is represented by doctrinal agreement about matters of truth. The weak form by what, in contrast, I shall call dialectical agreement about matters of truth.

In light of this statement of the problem to be solved and this indication of the key to its solution, I shall proceed as follows: First, to the consideration of truth itself, the difference between matters of truth and matters of taste, and the obligations we assume when we commit ourselves to the pursuit of truth within the confines of a single culture. Second, to the bearing of these considerations on the problem of cultural unity and cultural pluralism in the world as a whole with all its diverse cultures. In developing this we have to consider the irrefragable unity of the sphere of truth and the distinction between the strong and the weak forms of unity or agreement about matters that belong to the sphere of truth. Third, and last, to a summary of the conclusions to which we have been led.

The Pursuit of Truth

We must begin by asking, What is truth?

That is an easy question to which, in my judgment, there is only one right and tenable answer. The difficult question is not what is truth, but by what criteria can one determine the truth or falsity of the statements that men make or the opinions they hold. Knowing what truth is—what makes a statement or an opinion true—does not, by itself, enable us to tell whether a given statement or opinion is true or false. To answer the difficult question in detail would take more time than we have; in fact, would take several long lectures. But Pontius

Pilate would not have needed to wait long for an answer to the easy question.

You all know—at least implicitly—the answer, because you have all told lies and, perhaps, have even been caught telling them. To tell a lie, you must say in words the opposite of what you think to be the case. If you think that Kyoto has a smaller population than Tokyo, you would be telling a lie if you told a foreigner who asked about it that you thought its population was larger than Tokyo. It does not matter for the moment whether you are right or wrong in what you think about the relative population of Kyoto and Tokyo. Right or wrong, you are still telling a lie if you tell someone the opposite of what you know is the right answer to the question, and do so with the intention to deceive.

Or, to take another example, if you think that it is not raining at the present moment, you lie if you say to someone that you think it is. A lie consists in saying that something is the case when it is not the case or that something is not the case when it is the case. Josiah Royce quite correctly defined a liar as a person who willfully misplaces his ontological predicates—that is, a person who says "is" when he should say "is not" or says "is not" when he should say "is." Truth-telling as opposed to lying, prevarication, or falsity in speech can, therefore, be defined as the agreement of what one says with what one thinks about a given subject—what one believes or holds to be true about it.

This brings us to the question, What makes one's opinions or beliefs true or false? The answer parallels the answer to the question about the difference between truthful and untruthful speech. Just as truthful speech consists in the agreement between what you say and what you think, and untruthful speech consists in saying the opposite of what you think, so truth in what one thinks consists in the agreement between what one thinks and the way things really are. Conversely, falsity in what one thinks consists in the disagreement between what one thinks and the way things really are.

Aristotle summed this up in the following impeccable statement: To have truth in one's mind—in what one thinks, believes, or opines—consists in thinking that that which is, is, or that which is not, is not. Conversely, to have falsity in one's mind consists in thinking that that which is, is not, or that which is not, is. Thomas Aquinas said the same thing even more succinctly. He defined truth in the human intellect as the agreement or conformity of the mind with reality, and falsity as the opposite of that.

Underlying this definition of truth and falsity are two assumptions that Aristotle and Aquinas made, which, in my judgment, are philosophically defensible and tenable.

The first is that there exists a reality that is independent of the human mind, to which the mind can either conform or fail to conform. In other words, what we think does not create or in any way affect what we are thinking about. It is what it is, whether we think about it or not and regardless of what we think about it.

The second assumption is that this independent reality is completely determinate. This is Aristotle's metaphysical principle of contradiction. Nothing can both be and not be at the same time. Anything which does exist cannot both have and not have a certain attribute at one and the same time.

The metaphysical principle of contradiction gives rise to the logical principle which should govern our thought if we aim at the truth; namely, that we should not answer a question by saying both Yes and No to it at the same time. Or, put somewhat differently, we should not both affirm and deny the same proposition. We should not, for example, affirm that Socrates is a man and also deny that affirmation by asserting that Socrates is not a man.

This principle provides a complete refutation of the skeptic who declares that no statement is either true or false. For if the skeptic's declaration is true, then there is at least one statement which is true rather than false. And if it is false, then there may be many statements which are either true or false. And if it is neither true nor false, then why should we pay any attention to what the skeptic says?

Though I said earlier that I was not going to deal with the difficult question about how to determine the truth or falsity of particular statements, I have allowed myself, nevertheless, to assert the truth of the principle of contradiction as a basis for refuting the skeptic. How do I know that that statement is true? My answer is that we know that statement to be true because its truth is self-evident. It is evident to us from the very terms of the statement itself. Our understanding of the words "is" and "is not" is such that we cannot think the opposite of the principle of contradiction. We cannot think, at a given moment in time, that Socrates both does exist and does not exist. We cannot think, at a given moment in time, that Omaha both is and is not larger in population than Chicago.

One other illustration may make a little clearer the character of self-evident truths. Consider Euclid's axiom that a finite whole is greater than any of its parts, or that any part of a finite whole always is less than the whole. Now try to think the opposite: divide a piece of paper into quarters and try to think that the whole piece of paper was less than any of its parts, or that any of the quarters into which you divided the whole is greater than the original whole. For all other statements that we may affirm or deny—propositions that are not self-evident—determining whether they are true or false requires us to consider something other than the statement itself, which, as we have seen, is not required in the case of self-evident truths.

We may consider, for example, the truth of other statements and determine the truth of the statement in question by its relation to them. If the statement in question is inconsistent with other statements that we hold to be true, then that statement cannot itself be true. Or we may consider the evidence provided by our perceptual observations. If the statement in question is inconsistent with such evidence, then it is false, not true. Thus, when we observe one black swan, we know that the statement "All swans are white" is false.

I have permitted myself to go this far into the difficult matter of determining the truth or falsity of statements that are not self-evident—and I assure you it is not far enough— only in order to make one very important point. It is that, in the case of all statements that we judge to be true, whether they are self-evidently true or judged true by reference to other considerations, our judgment is necessitated, not voluntary or free. Just as we are not free to think the opposite of the self-evident truth that the whole is greater than any of its parts, so also we are not free to judge a proposition to be true if the weight of the evidence is against it or if the truth of other propositions is inconsistent with it.

The Difference Between Theoretical and Practical Truth

Aristotle's definition of truth holds only for statements that are descriptive; namely, statements that contain the words "is" or "is not," statements that assert that something is or is not the case.

What about the truth of normative statements, statements that contain the words "ought" or "ought not" instead of the words "is" and "is not," statements that assert that we ought to seek certain goals or that we ought to employ certain means for achieving them?

In modern times, the inability or failure to answer this

question has resulted in skepticism about moral knowledge; for if the definition of truth restricts its application to descriptive statements, then normative statements cannot be regarded as either true or false, in which case we cannot have any genuine knowledge—know the truth—about moral matters.

Consequently, ethics is regarded as noncognitive—that is, as falling outside the sphere of knowledge. What have come to be called "value judgments" (normative statements) are either expressions of emotion, of what I like or dislike, or of wishes, of what I want to do. Put another way, value judgments are purely matters of opinion, about which there is no point in arguing, as there is no point in arguing with someone who dislikes what you like, or who likes what you dislike.

Modern philosophers are totally unaware that Aristotle and Aquinas provided an answer to the question about the truth of value judgments as well as the answer to the question about the truth of descriptive statements or statements of fact. Recognizing that statements which contain the words "ought" and "ought not" cannot be true or false by their agreement or disagreement with reality, or with matters of fact, Aristotle said that such statements are true by another definition of truth. The truth of a prescriptive or normative statement—a statement saying what we ought or ought not to do—lies in its agreement with right desire, not in its agreement with reality. Right desire consists in desiring the things that are really good for us, as contrasted with the things that merely appear to be good for us and turn out to be really bad for us.

The first principle of ethics is that we ought to desire only the things that are really good for us. This first principle is self-evidently true. Test it for yourself as you tested the statement about wholes and parts. Just as you could not think of the whole as being less than any of its parts, so now you cannot think that you ought not to desire what is really good for you or that you ought to desire what is really bad for you.

APPENDICES

Beyond that first principle, you must of course acquire knowledge of what is and is not really good for you. When you know what is really good for you, you know what you ought to desire; and when you desire what you ought to desire, your desire is right; and so any statement to the effect that you ought to desire this or that conforms to right desire, and is true, if it is a statement that enjoins you to desire something that is really good for you.

We are all acquainted with the commonplace maxim: *de gustibus non disputandum est*. About matters of taste, we should not engage in arguments with one another. Why? Because we should not look for agreement about such matters. On the contrary, in this area we should gladly tolerate differences of opinion.

The very opposite maxim holds for matters of truth: *de veritate disputandum est*. Wherever the truth of statements, opinions, or beliefs is a proper concern, we should argue with one another. Argument is the means of resolving disagreements. When we disagree about matters of truth, we should seek agreement through argument. Disagreement about matters of truth is not, in the final reckoning, to be tolerated.

Let me make sure you understand what I am saying. I am not saying that, where the disagreement about a matter of truth is extremely difficult to resolve, we can achieve the agreement we ought to aim at within any specified period of time or by any devices available to us. I am only saying that we should never give up in our efforts to reach the agreement that we ought to aim at in a matter of truth. We may have to live with disagreements that cannot be resolved, but we should not regard them as ultimately tolerable.

As long as it is possible for us to carry on a rational process that is aimed at resolving a disagreement, our dedication to the pursuit of truth obliges us to proceed in that direction, never resting satisfied with anything less than the agreement of all that is the only appropriate condition of the human mind with regard to anything that is a matter of truth rather than a matter of taste.

To illustrate the difference between matters of truth and matters of taste, let me offer you some examples. There is a spectrum of matters some of which clearly belong to the sphere of truth and some as clearly to the sphere of taste. Let us start with clear cases at the extreme ends of the spectrum.

At one extreme, clearly belonging to the sphere of truth, is mathematics, and associated with it the exact sciences, especially the experimental sciences. Placing these disciplines in the sphere of truth does not mean that there is perfect agreement among all mathematicians or experimental scientists about everything in their fields. But it does mean, that, when they disagree, we expect them to be able to resolve their disagreements by rational processes. An irresolvable disagreement about any matter that properly falls in the sphere of truth would constitute an intellectual scandal. Not only would we find an irresolvable disagreement scandalous and intolerable, not only do we expect mathematicians and experimental scientists to be able to resolve whatever disagreements exist among them, but we also think that it is their obligation not to rest in their efforts to resolve such disagreements until they finally succeed in doing so.

At the opposite extreme, clearly belonging to the sphere of taste, are such matters as cuisine, social manners, styles in dress or dance, and so on. Here we do not expect that men should be able to resolve their differences in taste. We do not expect them to seek to achieve uniformity. On the contrary, we would regard as monstrous any attempt to impose conformity upon all to any one culinary program or set of social manners or style of dress. Here the adoption of one style rather than another is an act of free choice, not an act of the intellect necessitated by completely objective considerations.

Between these extremes, where there is no doubt that we are dealing with matters of truth on the one hand and with matters of taste on the other, philosophy and religion represent a difficult middle ground. The prevalent view today, in academic circles at least, tends to place philosophy and religion on the side of taste rather than on the side of truth. That has not always been the view taken about these subjects, nor is it necessarily the correct view to take of them.

With regard to the very difficult problem of locating the position of philosophy and religion on one or the other side of the line that divides matters of truth from matters of taste, I must content myself with just three brief observations.

First, whichever position one takes, the statement of that position itself should—I would almost say, must—be regarded as a judgment that is genuinely disputable, and therefore belongs to the sphere of truth rather than of taste. Second, I myself would advance the view, and be prepared to defend it by argument, either that philosophy and religion belong to the sphere of truth or that they are not worthy of intellectual respect and attention. And, assigning them to the sphere of truth, I would regard whatever disagreements exist in philosophical thought and in religious belief as resolvable, however difficult it may be to resolve them. Our obligation here, in the pursuit of truth, is to be tireless and unrelenting in our efforts to resolve them.

In addition to the questionable middle ground occupied by philosophy and religion in the spectrum of matters that fall between the poles of what is clearly truth and what is clearly taste, there are some matters which combine the elements of both truth and taste. The customs of a society, its political and economic institutions, and above all its positive laws, are prime examples of mixtures of truth and taste.

The best way to understand why this mixture occurs is to see that such matters involve both the natural and the conventional, both the necessary and the contingent, both the rational and the voluntary. Positive laws, for example, insofar as they have some basis in the natural moral law or in principles of natural justice, have an element of truth about them. But insofar as they also involve voluntarily instituted determinations of the natural moral law, devised to accord with the contingent circumstances of a particular society at a particular time, an element of taste enters in to their adoption.

The important point to observe with respect to these mixtures of truth and taste is that whatever is to the slightest degree infected by taste must be placed on the side of taste rather than on the side of truth. This is simply to say that, while it is reasonable to expect agreement about the precepts of the natural moral law, it would be unreasonable to expect uniformity in rules of positive law. We should not expect all societies to adopt the same rules of positive law, nor should we expect them to make any effort to resolve their legislative differences. The only uniformity we should expect to find in the diverse codes of positive law enacted by different states derives from the substratum of natural law or natural justice that should be common to all of them.

Cultural Unity and Cultural Pluralism

I turn now to the bearing of the points so far considered on the problem of cultural unity and cultural pluralism. Two things should be immediately obvious.

There is no question about worldwide cultural unity with regard to mathematics and the exact and experimental sciences. We have already achieved a high degree of transcultural agreement in these fields, and we should expect it to continue and approach completeness. Nor is there any question about worldwide cultural unity with respect to the principles of technology that underlie the products of technology that are now also transcultural—adopted worldwide. Unity with respect to these principles is, after all, nothing but an extension by application of the agreements achieved in mathematics and the exact sciences.

Tabling for the moment the insistent question about the status of philosophy and religion, we can say that in all other matters, which are matters of taste, we should both expect and tolerate cultural diversity and pluralism even in a world community when that comes into existence. This holds for the clear cases already mentioned, such things as cuisine, social manners, styles of dress and dance, and so forth.

It also holds for what I have called mixtures of truth and taste, of the natural and the conventional, such as rules of positive law. If the government of a world community were federal in structure, we should expect and tolerate pluralism in the codes of positive law adopted by the units in the federal system. A world federal constitution will demand agreement from local codes of positive law only to the extent that the federal constitution includes a bill of human or natural rights, the violation of which would be nullified as unconstitutional. . . .

Since it is only in the spheres of mathematics and experimental science that doctrinal agreement has been achieved in large measure, if not completely, the truth agreed upon in those areas at a given time tests the claims to truth that are made in philosophy and religion—areas in which doctrinal agreement has not been achieved to any appreciable degree.

In other words, a particular religious belief or philosophical view must be rejected as false if, at a given time, it comes into conflict with the scientific truths agreed upon at that time.

We are now in a position to carry the argument out in some detail. To say that there is one whole of truth all the parts of which must coherently and consistently fit together does not preclude the parts from being different from one another in a variety of ways—with respect to the objects with which they are concerned, with respect to the methods by which inquiry is conducted, and with respect to the sources or bases of the truth being sought. No matter how diverse may be the objects, methods, and sources involved in the different parts of truth, they all remain, nevertheless, parts of one whole, and as such they must coherently and consistently fit together.

Wherever the fruits of technology are used or enjoyed, the truth of science and mathematics is acknowledged. The fruits of technology are now enjoyed all over the world—in the Far East as well as the West. It follows, therefore, that the truth of science and mathematics is acknowledged all over the world. It is the only part of the whole truth that is common to the Far East and the West.

The same mandate that has been operative within the Western tradition should, therefore, be operative when we go beyond the Western tradition and consider the philosophies and religions of the Far East as well as the philosophies and religions of the West. Just as, within the Western tradition, the truths of mathematics and science that are agreed upon at a given time have been employed as the test for accepting or rejecting Western beliefs or philosophical views, so, in exactly the same way, they should be employed as the test for accepting or rejecting Far Eastern religious beliefs or philosophical views.

The principle that whatever is inconsistent or incompatible with the truths of mathematics and science that are agreed upon at a given time must, at that time, be rejected as false is universally applicable—to Eastern as well as to Western culture.

142

There are only two ways in which this consequence can be avoided. One is to deny the principle of contradiction and, with it, the unity of truth. The other is to regard Eastern religions and philosophies as making no cognitive claims at all, thus putting them along with cuisine, dress, manners, and customs on the side of taste rather than on the side of truth. . . .

When we turn from the West to the whole world, and particularly to the Far Eastern cultures in relation to one another as well as to the West, the situation is not the same. There is not one dialogue being carried on, nor one universe of discourse embracing all who are engaged in the pursuit of philosophical truth.

Agreement does not exist as between the Far East and West: nor for that matter does it exist between any one of the major Far Eastern cultures and any of the others. The reason why it does not exist may be that none of the Far Eastern cultures claims truth for its philosophical doctrines. If that is the case, then, as I have said before, there is no problem. Eastern philosophies, unlike Western philosophies, must then be regarded as matters of taste rather than truth. They do not conflict with one another or with Western philosophical thought in a way that requires resolution, any more than differences in cuisine conflict with one another and require resolution.

However, if the several Far Eastern cultures regard philosophy as an area in which the criteria of truth and falsity are applicable, and if the criteria are operative in the same way in philosophy as they are in science and mathematics, then it must be possible to establish a measure of logical agreement, as between the Far East and the West as well as between the several Far Eastern cultures, a measure sufficient to make some progress toward resolving the doctrinal disagreements that exist.

APPENDICES

Let me repeat the point that constitutes the nerve of my argument. The fruits of technology are now universally put to use. This confirms the universal acknowledgment of a worldwide transcultural agreement about the best approximations to truth that we have made so far in mathematics and experimental science.

That agreement involves an agreement about the rules of logic and of discourse which enable men to pursue the truth cooperatively and to resolve their doctrinal disagreements. The logic of science and of mathematics is, like science and mathematics, global, not Western.

Though the method of philosophy may not be the same as that of mathematics or science, the basic framework of its logic is the same. A contradiction is a contradiction whether it occurs in philosophy, in mathematics, or in science. Unchecked equivocation in the use of words generates fallacious arguments, whether in philosophy or in science and mathematics. This is my basis for saying that a dialectical agreement at least should be achievable worldwide in the sphere of philosophy. Please note that I said "achievable." It does not exist at present to any appreciable degree.

The problem of religion is more difficult than that of philosophy. If religion claims to involve knowledge, then we must face a further question. Is it indistinguishable from philosophy as a branch of natural knowledge, or does it regard itself as quite distinct from philosophy and all other branches of natural knowledge because it and it alone has its source in divine revelation, accepted by an act of faith that is itself divinely caused? In the latter case, religion claims to be supernatural knowledge—knowledge that man has only as a gift from God. In contrast, natural knowledge, in all its branches, consists of knowledge that man acquires by the exercise of the powers of observation and thought with which he is naturally endowed.

Human Nature, Nurture, and Culture

(Excerpts from a Lecture Delivered at the
Aspen Institute in 1989)

(1)

. . . I must begin by commenting on an extraordinary error made by twentieth-century social scientists and by the existentialist philosophy that arose in France in this century. It consists in denying that man has a specific nature comparable to the specific natures to be found in the zoological taxonomy—in the classification of animals according to their generic and specific natures. As the existentialists put it, man has an existence but no essence: the essence of each human being is of his or her own making. As the social scientists put it, the differences among human groups—racial, ethnic, or cultural—are primary; there is no common human nature in which they all share. The French existentialist Maurice Merleau-Ponty sums up this error by saying: "It is the nature of man not to have a nature."

Before I explain how this profound mistake came to be made,

145

let me call your attention to its serious consequences. If moral philosophy is to have a sound factual basis, it is to be found in the facts about human nature and nowhere else. Nothing else but the sameness of human nature at all times and places, from the beginning of homo sapiens 45,000 years ago, can provide the basis for a set of moral values that should be universally accepted. Nothing else will correct the mistaken notion that we should readily accept a pluralism of moral values as we pass from one human group to another or within the same human group. If the basis in human nature for a universal ethic is denied, the only other alternative lies in the extreme rationalism of Immanuel Kant, which proceeds without any consideration of the facts of human life and with no concern for the variety of cases to which moral prescriptions must be applied in a manner that is flexible rather than rigorous.

I turn now to the explanation of the mistaken denial of human nature, which while conceding that all human beings have certain common anatomical and physiological traits— number of bones, number of teeth, blood type, number of chromosomes, the period of parturition, and so on—denies their psychological sameness, the sameness of the human mind and its behavioral tendencies. How was that mistake made?

Consider other animal species. If you were to investigate any one of them as carefully as possible, you would find that the members of the same species, living in their natural habitats, manifest a remarkable degree of similarity in behavior. You might find difference in size, weight, shape, or coloration among the individuals you examined. You might find behavioral deviations here and there from what would have become evident as the normal behavior of that species. But, by and large, you would be impressed by the similitudes that reigned in the populations you examined.

The dominant likeness of all members of the species would

lead you to dismiss as relatively insignificant the differences you found, most of which can be explained as the result of slightly different environmental conditions. That dominant likeness would constitute the nature of the species in question.

Now consider the human species. It inhabits the globe. Its members live in all hemispheres and regions, under the most widely divergent environmental conditions. Let us suppose you were to take the time to visit human populations wherever they existed—all of them. Let the visit not be a casual one, but one in which you lived for a time with each of these populations and studied them closely. You would come away with the very opposite impression from the one you took away from your investigation of the populations that belonged to one or another animal species. You were there impressed by the overwhelming similitude that reigned among its members. Here, however, you would find that the behavioral differences were dominant rather than the similarities.

Of course human beings, like other animals, must eat, drink, and sleep. They all have certain biological traits in common. There can be no doubt that they have the nature of animals. But when you come to their distinctive behavioral traits, how different one human population will be from another. They will differ in the languages they speak, and you will have some difficulty in making an accurate count of the vast number of different languages you will have found. They will differ in their dress, in their adornments, in their cuisines, in their customs and manners, in the organization of their families, in the institutions of their societies, in their beliefs, in their standards of conduct, in the turn of their minds, in almost everything that enters into the ways of life they lead. These differences will be so multitudinous and variegated that you might, unless cautioned against doing so, tend to be persuaded that they were not all members of the same species.

In any case, you cannot avoid being persuaded that, in the human case, membership in the same species does not carry with it the dominant behavioral similitude that you would find in the case of other animal species. On the contrary, the behavioral differences between one human race and another, between one racial variety and another, between one ethnic group and another, between one nation and another, would seem to be dominant.

It is this that might lead you to the conclusion that there is no human nature in the sense in which a certain constant nature can be attributed to other species of animals. Even if you did not reach the conclusion yourself, you might understand how that conclusion is plausible.

Unlike most other species of animals, the members of the human species appear to have formed subgroups that differentiated themselves, one from another. Each subgroup has a distinctive character. The differences that separate one subgroup from another are so numerous and so profound that they defy you to say what remains, if anything, that might be regarded as a human nature common to all.

Let me be sure it is understood that the denial of human nature rests ultimately on the striking contrast between the dominant behavioral similitude that prevails among the members of other animal species and the dominant behavioral differentiation that prevails among the subgroups of the human species.

Looked at one way, the denial of human nature is correct. The members of the human species do not have a specific or common nature *in the same sense* that the members of other animal species do. This, by the way, is one of the most remarkable differences between man and other animals, one that tends to corroborate the conclusion that man differs from other animals in kind, not in degree. But to concede that the members of the human species do not have a specific or common nature *in the same sense* that the members of other animal species do is not to admit that they have *no specific nature whatsoever*.

An alternative remains open; namely, that the members of the human species all have the same nature in a quite different sense.

In what sense then is there a human nature, a specific nature that is common to all members of the species? The answer can be given in a single word: *potentialities*. Human nature is constituted by all the potentialities that are the species-specific properties common to all members of the human species.

It is the essence of a potentiality to be capable of a wide variety of different actualizations. Thus, for example, the human potentiality for syntactical speech is actualized in thousands of different human languages. Having that potentiality a human infant placed at the moment of birth in one or another human subgroup, each with its own language, would learn to speak that language. The differences among all human languages are superficial as compared with the potentiality for learning and speaking any human language that is present in all human infants at birth.

What has just been said about one human potentiality applies to all the others that are the common, specific traits of the human being. Each underlies all the differences that arise among human subgroups as a result of the many different ways in which the same potentiality can be actualized. To recognize this is tantamount to acknowledging the superficiality of the differences that separate one human subgroup from another, as compared with the samenesses that unite all human beings as members of the same species and as having the same specific nature.

In other species of animals, the samenesses that unite the members and constitute their common nature are not potentialities but rather quite determinate characteristics, behavioral as well as anatomical and physiological. This accounts for the impression derived from studying these other species—the impression of a dominant similitude among its members.

Turning to the human species, the opposite impression of dominant differences among subgroups can also be accounted for. The explanation of it lies in the fact that, as far as behavioral characteristics are concerned, the common nature that all the subgroups share consists entirely of species-specific potentialities. These are actualized by these subgroups in all the different ways that we find when we make a global study of mankind.

The mistake that the cultural anthropologists, the sociologists, and other behavioral scientists make when they deny the existence of human nature has its roots in their failure to understand that the specific nature in the case of the human species is radically different from the specific nature in the case of other animal species.

Having established the sameness of the human species, which consists in its common human potentialities, psychological and behavioral, in addition to its common anatomical and physiological traits, let us now consider the difference between the human species and other animal species.

(2)

That we differ from other, nonhuman animals in many respects is doubted by no one. But among these differences are *some* differences in kind, or are *all* differences in degree? Differences in degree are all differences of more and less with respect to the same property or trait. For example, all animals mature from infancy at different rates, humans more slowly than other animals. That is a difference in degree. Two things differ in kind rather than degree if one has a property that the other totally lacks: it is a difference between *haves* and *have nots*. For example, the difference between animals that have and lack backbones is a difference in kind.

In a book published in 1967, *The Difference of Man and the Difference It Makes*, and in a book published in 1990, *Intellect: Mind Over Matter*, I think I have shown, beyond a reasonable doubt, that mentally and behaviorally, human beings differ in kind from nonhuman animals. All the differences between humans and nonhumans are not differences in degree.

I shall not state all these differences in kind, but only the most important and obvious ones.

Intellect is a unique human possession. Only human beings have intellects. Other animals may have sensitive minds and perceptual intelligence, but they do not have intellects. No one is given to saying that dogs and cats, horses, pigs, dolphins, and chimpanzees lead intellectual lives; nor do we say of nonhuman animals that they are anti-intellectual, as some human beings certainly are. Other animals have intelligence in varying degrees, but they do not have intellectual powers in the least degree.

Free will or free choice, which consists in always being able to choose otherwise, no matter how one does choose, is an intellectual property, lacked by nonintellectual animals. Some of their behavior may be learned and thus acquired rather than innate and instinctive, but however it is determined by instinct or by learning, it is *determined* rather than *voluntary* and *freely willed*.

A person is a living being with intellect and free will. That is both the jurisprudential and the theological definition of a person. Everything else, animate or inanimate, totally lacking intellect and free will, is not a person but a thing.

Only persons have natural and unalienable rights. These we call

151

human rights. There are no comparable animal rights. Morally, human beings may be obliged to treat some, but not all, other animals humanely. For example, we are not obliged to treat humanely a coiled rattlesnake about to strike or a charging tiger.

In addition to the foregoing basic differences in kind between human and nonhuman animals, there are the following behavioral differences in kind.

Other animals live entirely in the present. Only human individuals are time-binders, connecting the present with the remembered past and with the imaginable future. Only man is a historical animal with a historical tradition and a historical development. In the case of other species, the life of succeeding generations remains the same as long as no genetic changes occur. Human life changes from one generation to another with the transmission of cultural novelties and with accretion of accumulated cultural changes and institutional innovations. Nothing like these innovations and changes can be found in any other species.

Other animals make things, such as hives, nests, dams, and, in the case of birds, songs. It may even be that in doing so, other animals use rudimentary tools as well as their own appendages.

But only man makes machines, which are not hand tools, for the purpose of making products that cannot be produced in any other way. It is not enough to say that man is the only manufacturing animal. We must add that he is the only machinofacturing animal. The kind of thought that is involved in designing and building a machine betokens the presence of an intellect in a way that the use of hand tools does not.

Among the things that man makes are works of art that we regard as fine rather than useful because they are made for the pleasure or enjoyment they afford rather than to serve some further purpose. Are the songs made by birds comparable? No, because even if the songs birds make serve no biological purpose and are simply made to be enjoyed, the songs made by a given species of bird remain the same for all members of that species generation after generation. In contrast, in the making of drawings or paintings, from the sketches drawn on the walls of the Cro-Magnon caves down to the present day, the extraordinary variety in human works of art shows that human artistry is not instinctive, and therefore not the same for all members of the species from one generation to the other.

As I see it, all the differences in kind so far mentioned cannot be explained except by reference to man's exclusive possession of an intellect, with its power of conceptual thought and its power of free choice. If any doubt about man's difference in kind remains in your minds, let me try to persuade you by the following distinctive, unique human performances that I think you will find unquestionable.

Only human beings use their minds to become artists, historians, philosophers, priests, teachers, lawyers, physicians, engineers, accountants, inventors, traders, bankers, statesmen.

Only among human beings is there a distinction between those who behave ethically and those who are knaves, scoundrels, villains, criminals.

Only among human beings is there any distinction between those who have mental health and those who suffer mental disease or have mental disabilities of one sort or another.

Only in the sphere of human life are there such institutions as schools, libraries, hospitals, churches, temples, factories, prisons, cemeteries, and so on. . . .

(3)

What is the role of nurture in human life?

All the knowledge we acquire, all the understanding we

develop, everything we learn, is a product of nurture. At birth, we have none of these. All the habits we form, all the tastes we cultivate, all the patterns of behavior we accumulate are products of nurture. We are born only with potentialities or powers that are habituated by the things we do in the course of growing up. Many, if not all, of these habits of behavior are acquired under the influence of the homes and families, the tribes and/or societies in which we are brought up. Some are the results of individually chosen behavior.

What nurture adds to nature in the development of human beings should be so clear to all of us that we do not make the serious mistake that results from the failure to distinguish what human nature is from all of its nurtural overlays. That serious mistake has been made again and again during the last four thousand years. We found it being made in the twentieth century by those sociologists and existentialists who deny the existence of human nature itself because of the pluralism they find in differently nurtured groups of human beings. Equally serious is the mistake of regarding human inequalities that result from nurtural influences as if they were the manifestation of unequal natural endowments.

To be sure this is clear, let me repeat once more the difference between human nature and that of all other animal species. In the case of other animal species, the specific nature common to all members of the species is constituted mainly by quite determinable characteristics or attributes. In the case of the human species, it is constituted by determinable characteristics or attributes. An innate potentiality is precisely that: something determinable, not wholly determinate, and determinable in a wide variety of ways.

Man is to a great extent a self-made creature. Given a range of potentialities at birth, he makes himself what he becomes by how he freely chooses to develop those potentialities by the

154

habits he forms. It is thus that differentiated subgroups of human beings came into existence. Once in existence, they subsequently affected the way in which those born into these subgroups came to develop the acquired characteristics that differentiate one subgroup from another. These acquired characteristics, especially the behavioral ones, are the results of acculturation; or, even more generally, results of the way in which those born into this or that subgroup are nurtured differently.

No other animal is a self-made creature in the sense indicated above. On the contrary, other animals have determinate natures, natures genetically determined in such a way that they do not admit of a wide variety of different developments as they mature. Human nature is also genetically determined; but because the genetic determination consists, behaviorally, in an innate endowment of potentialities that are determinable in different ways, human beings differ remarkably from one another as they mature. However they originated in the first place, most of those differences are due to differences in acculturation, to natural differences. To confuse nature with nurture is a philosophical mistake of the first order. And that philosophical mistake underlies the denial of human nature. . . .

The correction of the mistake that confuses nature with nurture leads to certain conclusions that many individuals may find disconcerting. All the cultural and nurtural differences that separate one human subgroup from another are superficial as compared with the underlying common human nature that unites the members of mankind.

Although our samenesses are more important than our differences, we have an inveterate tendency to stress the differences that divide us rather than the samenesses that unite us. We find it difficult to believe that the human mind is the same

155

everywhere because we fail to realize that all the differences, however striking, between the mind of Western man and the mind of human beings nurtured in the various Eastern cultures are, in the last analysis, superficial—entirely the result of different nurturing.

If a world cultural community is ever to come into existence, it will retain cultural pluralism or diversity with respect to all matters that are accidental in human life, such things as cuisine, dress, manners, customs, and the like. These are the things that vary from one human subgroup to another accordingly as these subgroups differ in the way they nurture their members. When that happens, we will have at last overcome the illusion that there is a Western mind and an Eastern mind, a European mind and an African mind, or a civilized mind and a primitive mind. There is only a human mind and it is one and the same in all human beings.

INDEX

157

INDEX

INDEX

Freud, Sigmund, 83
Fundamentalism, 60*n*, 64, 65

Galileo, 96
Genesis, demythologizing of, 65–66
Germanic mythology, 53
Gill, Brendan, 59*n*
God
  argument affirming existence of,
    18, 19, 37, 48, 107–108
  Campbell on, 58–60
  Cox on, 81
  creation of universe by, 26–27, 65
  kingdom of, 80
  knowledge given by, 51
  Plato on, 54
  as a purely spiritual being, 35
  revealed word of, 29, 70
  self-revelation of, 109
Golden Bough, The (Frazer), 42
Golden Rule, 87–88
Grammar of Assent (Newman), 41
Greek mythology, 53–54
Greek philosophy, 70–71. *See also*
  Artistotle; Plato

Hardy, G. H., 99*n*
Hassidic Jews, 40
Hawking, Stephen, 14, 71
Hegel, Georg, 43, 82
Heidegger, Martin, 83
Heisenberg, Werner, 71, 93, 94*n*,
  95, 118
Hero with a Thousand Faces, The
  (Campbell), 38
Hesiod, 53
Hinduism, 48, 49, 69, 82
  moral laws of, 87
Historical research, 27, 33, 104
Hobbes, Thomas, 96
Homer, 53
How to Think About God (Adler), 18*n*,
  107
Human mind
  reality and, 133

species-specific properties of, 113–
  14, 128–30, 146, 155–56
  truth and, 116, 117
Human nature, 145–56
Hume, David, 43

Icelandic mythology, 53
Idealistic philosophy, 22, 71, 74, 99
Immortality of soul, 31–32
Indeterminacy and Indeterminability,
  93–99
Inner Reaches of Outer Space, The
  (Campbell), 58, 59*n*
Intellect, immateriality of, 31–32
Intellect: Mind Over Matter (Adler),
  22*n*, 151
Islam, 48, 49, 59*n*, 82, 104, 108–110
  Aristotelian philosophy and, 24
  articles of faith in, 18
  creation in, 65
  dogmatic theology and, 41–42
  Greek philosophy and, 70
  moral laws of, 87
  study of, 40

Jainism, 48, 87
James, William, 22–23, 44*n*
Jesus Christ, 80, 81
  dual nature of, 18
  historical, 38–39
  moral teachings of, 87
John, St., 80
Judaism, 48, 49, 59, 103, 108–110
  articles of faith in, 18, 26–27
  creation in, 65
  dogmatic theology and, 41–42
  Greek philosophy and, 70
  moral laws of, 87
  study of, 40
Judgments, 12–13
  uncertainty of, 16–17
Jung, Carl, 83

Kant, Immanuel, 43, 82, 146
Koran, 19
Küng, Hans, 79, 81–86, 101

159

INDEX

INDEX

Philosophical truth, 27–28, 30, 31, 33–35, 72, 89, 102
Philosophy
  atomic theory and, 96–100
  dialectical agreement in, 120, 144
  Eastern, 70, 142–43
  in Middle Ages, 90
  moral, 46
  of religion, 43–45
  scholastic, 41
  transcultural, 5, 104, 106, 107
Physics, 71, 75–76, 94, 97. *See also*
  Quantum physics
Piaget, Jean, 114
Plato, 53–55, 58*n*, 116
Poetical truth, 11–12, 25–26, 39, 102, 103, 105
  in Eastern religions, 73
  in mythology, 11, 25, 39, 53, 55–57, 61, 63, 64, 84, 85, 89
Poetics (Aristotle), 25, 68
Political philosophy, 120
Political pluralism, 2, 7–9, 101–102
Polytheism, 47, 49, 106
  mythology and, 53
Positive law, rules of, 141
Potentialities, species–specific, 149
Power of Myth, The (Campbell), 59*n*
Practical truth, 135–40
Pragmatic theory of truth, 22–23
Preceptorial religions, 47, 48
Prescriptive truth, 20–22, 86–89
Priesthood, separation of laity and, 46
Promised Land, 58, 60
Proselytizing, 79, 108
Protestantism, 79, 82

Quakers, 46
Quantum theory and reality, 71, 93–100, 117

Raschke, Carl, 81
Rational inquiry, 17–18
Reality, correspondence of truth with, 22–23
  and quantum theory, 93–99

Reasonableness of Christianity, The (Locke), 41
Religious law, code of, 46
Renan, Ernest, 38
Republic (Plato), 53
Resurrection, 59
Revealed truth, 29
Rhetorical attacks on religious beliefs, 37–39
Roman Catholicism, 33, 79, 82
Roman mythology, 53
Roszak, Theodore, 126–27
Royce, Josiah, 116, 132

Sacraments, 41
Sacred, separation of profane and, 45–46, 90
Santayana, George, 61
Schleiermacher, Friedrich, 43
Scholastic philosophy, 41
Schopenhauer, Arthur, 83
Schrödinger, Erwin, 95*n*
Science, 13, 30, 31, 33–34, 72, 74, 75, 83, 102, 104, 106, 120, 122–24, 126, 138, 142, 144
Scriptures, 28–30, 34, 60*n*, 65–67
Self-evident truths, 20, 72, 116–17, 136
Shintoism, 48, 49, 69
Sikhism, 48
Six Great Ideas (Adler), 13*n*, 22
Sociology, 42, 62
Sociology of Religion, The (Weber), 42
Sophocles, 11
Soul, immortality of, 31–32
Species-specific properties, 113–14, 128, 129, 145–56
Spinoza, Benedict, 26–27
Strong disjunctions, 15–16
Structuralism, 114
Subatomic reality, 94–99, 118
Subjective versus objective, 126–27
Summa Theologica (Aquinas), 41*n*
Supernatural knowledge, 51–52, 90, 104
Superstition, 65, 102

INDEX

Taoism, 48, 49, 69, 87
Taste, matters of, 2–4, 6, 11, 101, 119–21, 130, 131, 137–41, 143
Technology, 4, 31, 34, 73–77, 104, 106, 120, 123, 126, 141, 142
Ten Commandments, 19
Tertullian, 18–19
Theological religions, 47–49, 52, 107
Theology
  dogmatic, 41–42, 44, 90
  philosophical, 14, 18, 77, 91–92, 107
Theology for the Third Millennium: An Ecumenical View (Küng), 79
Theoretical truth, 135–40
Thought-experiments, 95
Timaeus (Plato), 55
Time, measurable, 14, 71
Tolerance, 1, 3
  Mill on, 5–6
Totalitarian regimentation, 3
Toynbee, Arnold, 89
Transculturality, principle of, 106, 107
Triune nature of Godhead, 18

Uncertainty principle, 71–72, 93, 95, 118
Unity of truth, principle of, 105, 107, 115–16, 118, 119, 121, 130, 143
Universe. *See* Cosmos

Value judgments, 136
Values, 4
Varieties of Religious Experience, The (James), 44n
Virgin Birth, 58, 60
Voltaire, 37

Wave-particle duality, 93
Weak disjunctions, 15
Weber, Max, 42
Where the Wasteland Ends (Roszak), 126
World government, 89, 114–15, 130
World peace, 114–15, 128, 130
Worship, 45

Yeshiva schools, 40

Zen Buddhism, 75–76